The New Temple Shakespeare

Edited by M. R. RIDLEY, M.A.

KING RICHARD III

by William Shakespeare

6697

J. M. DENT & SONS LTD., London
E. P. DUTTON & CO., INC., New York

Editor's General Note

THE TEXT. The editor has kept before him the aim of presenting to the modern reader the nearest possible approximation to what Shakespeare actually wrote. The text is therefore conservative, and is based on the earliest reliable printed text. But to avoid distraction (a) the spelling is modernised, and (b) a limited number of universally accepted emendations is admitted without comment. Where a Quarto text exists as well as the First Folio the passages which occur only in the Quarto are enclosed in square brackets [ ] and those which occur only in the Folio in brace brackets { }.

SCENE DIVISION. The rapid continuity of the Elizabethan curtainless production is lost by the 'traditional' scene divisions. Where there is an essential difference of place these scene divisions are retained. Where on the other hand the change of place is insignificant the scene division is indicated only by a space on the page. For ease of reference, however, the 'traditional' division is retained at the head of the page and in line numbering.

NOTES. Passages on which there are notes are indicated by a † in the margin.

PUNCTUATION adheres more closely than has been usual to the 'Elizabethan' punctuation of the early texts. It is often therefore more indicative of the way in which the lines were to be delivered than of their syntactical construction.

GLOSSARIES are arranged on a somewhat novel principle, not alphabetically, but in the order in which the words or phrases occur. The editor is much indebted to Mr. J. N. Bryson for his collaboration in the preparation of the glossaries.

Preface

THE TEXT. The First Quarto was published in 1597, with the title-page:—THE TRAGEDY OF / King Richard the third. / Containing, / His treacherous Plots against his brother Clarence: / the pittieful murther of his innocent nephewes: / his tyrannical vsurpation: with the whole course / of his detested life, and most deserued death. / As it hath beene lately Acted by the / Right honourable the Lord Chamber- / laine his seruants. / AT LONDON / Printed by Valentine Sims, for Andrew Wise, / dwelling in Paules Church-yard, at the / Signe of the Angell. / 1597.

In the Second Quarto (1598) the author's name is added. The Third Quarto (1602) advertises itself as "Newly augmented," but the only augmentation it exhibits is in the number of errors. Three more Quartos followed before the Folio, in 1605, 1612, 1622.

The problem of the text of the play is unhappily very intricate. The facts are not in dispute. The Quartos as a block represent one text of the play, with the usual feature that the number of errors increases with each succeeding quarto; the Folio represents another text, which is not only longer, but different. In the first place there are about 200 lines (as well as a certain number of half lines) in F which do not appear in Q at all; while there are some 25 lines (as well as some half lines) which occur only in Q, about two-thirds of them being accounted for by one passage, IV. ii. 103–21. There is a certain number of passages in which the substance is the same in Q and F but the form is different, Q as a rule being the rougher and metrically the less satisfactory. Further, the stage-directions of F are the fuller, and certain minor parts which appear in F do not appear in Q. So far there is no feature which cannot be paralleled in other plays and accounted for on the supposition that both texts are derived from the same original MS., which is represented in its 'cut' form by Q and in its uncut form, somewhat edited, by F; though, even so, it will be found on examination that an inconveniently high proportion of the 'F only' lines are single lines whose absence in Q does not, on the face of it, look like the result of dramatic cutting. But when we come to a collation of Q and F a much more unusual and puzzling feature presents itself. There is throughout the play, except in three passages of some length (I. i., III. i., and V. iii. 45 to the end of the play), a very large number of verbal differences which present this peculiarity: they are quite definite (*i.e.*, they cannot be due to a misreading by one or other compositor or transcriber of the same original), but also they are mostly unimportant. A few instances will illustrate their nature:

'*As* miserable by the death of him
 As I am made by my *poor* lord and thee' (Q)
'*More* miserable by the death of him
 Than I am made by my *young* lord and thee' (F)

'*Some* score or two' (Q)
'A score or two' (F)

'him that *slew* my husband' (Q)
'him that *kill'd* my husband' (F)

and a large number of similar pairs, *throw, hurl; heart, soul; perform'd, dispatch'd; scorned, flouted; laments, complaints; dread, fear; bad, ill;* and so on without end. There is a number of transpositions, such as *carping censures of the world, censures of the carping world; innocent alabaster, alabaster innocent.*

Then there is a smaller number of instances which seem to be more significant; either F cures a halting metre,

'*Came* from visiting his majesty' (Q)
'*Are come* from visiting his majesty' (F)

or it removes an awkwardness of expression,

'thus taunted scorn'd and baited at' (Q)
'so baited scorn'd and stormed at' (F)

or it avoids (for better or worse) a repetition,

'Your eyes drop millstones when fools' eyes *drop* tears' (Q)
'Your eyes drop millstones when fools' eyes *fall* tears' (F)

'Methought that Gloster stumbled and in *stumbling*' (Q)
'Methought that Gloster stumbled and in *falling*' (F)

or it uses the more ordinary for the less ordinary word,

'and then we will *chop* him *in* the malmsey butt' (Q)
'and then *throw* him *into* the malmsey butt' (F).

Of some 550 such verbal differences noted in collating (very far
from an exhaustive list) all but 40 show a coincidence of the six
Quartos against the Folio. Into the intricacies of the differences
between the various Quartos and the possible relation of the
Folio to any one of them (why, for example, of the 40 instances
just mentioned 23 are concentrated in 250 lines of one scene)
there is no space here to enter, but the main significant facts are
as stated above, and make it clear that we are dealing with two
texts. But as to the interpretation of those facts there has been a
sharp divergence of opinion. One school of critics maintains that
Q represents Shakespeare's original text, F a revision and en-
largement of it, whether by Shakespeare or by someone else; the
other that F represents the original form, shortened and revised
(whether for better or worse) into Q. The Cambridge editors,
for example, assumed that Q was printed from a transcript of the
original MS., that later Shakespeare revised and enlarged this
MS., that another transcript was made of this revised MS. and
that F was printed from this second transcript. To account for
the verbal differences they had to assume that this second transcriber had an ill-controlled passion for trivial alteration. Daniel,
on the other hand, thinks that F is the original text, of which Q
is a cut and altered version, and that F was printed from a copy
of Q 6, corrected by the original MS.[1]

[1] There are no doubt some instances, though not, I think, nearly so many
as Daniel supposes (since it is not beyond the reach of easy coincidence that
if Q 6 makes an error printing from Q 5, F may make the same error printing

One of the difficulties in the problem is that the disputants are, I think, too whole-heartedly and exclusively attached to their own particular views, and not ready enough to admit that different sets of facts seem to point in different directions, that different types of divergence between Q and F may be due to different causes. For example, it seems highly unlikely that the long passages peculiar to F were later insertions, since there seems no reason why anyone should take the trouble to insert them; so far as they are concerned we naturally assume F to be the original and Q the cut original. Many of the single lines peculiar to F might well be later insertions, so that on their evidence we might assume Q to be the original and F the revision, but readily admitting the possibility of the converse. On the other hand a number of the differences seem to show F at its usual process of editing and tidying and polishing, and so point to Q as the original. Lastly, a great proportion of the verbal differences seem to me to belong to a different order altogether, and have nothing to do with the rest of the evidence. They are exactly the kind of error that is made by the actor who has learnt his part in a hurry and is not word-perfect; he retains the sense and the metre, but transposes the order of words or substitutes rough equivalents. It is, of course, impossible to prove that these differences are not the result of revision, but it is hard to conceive of anyone taking the trouble to make so many alterations of this particular type. And it is noticeable that the differences of this type are apt to come in blocks, and in the comparatively unimportant speech openings and endings. In fact, so far as these verbal differences are concerned, whichever text we assume to be the original, the other bears the characteristic marks of a 'reported' (though unusually well-reported) text. And the moment that not only the peculiar character, but also the number, of these divergences is appreciated, the problem is seen to be yet more complicated, since they point to some

---

from MS.), which make it likely that F had some connection with Q 6. But I do not think that Daniel gives any explanation why, if the original MS. was available, anyone should be at the trouble (and, so far as inserted passages go, the mechanically awkward trouble) of inserting in a printed text many hundreds (400 odd in the first act alone, and not less than 2000 in the whole play) of alterations, mostly trivial, instead of handing over the MS. to be printed from direct.

stage in transmission where the source of error was someone's memory. They are not the errors that would be made by an ordinary transcriber, adhering as best he could to an unfamiliar manuscript; but they are exactly the errors which might be made by someone transcribing a MS. with which he was familiar, most particularly if he was also familiar with it as delivered on the stage. I feel that Sir Edmund Chambers shows at least not less than his usual temperate wisdom in his comments. (He is assuming that his suggested transcript was the basis of Q, but I think that it is at least possible that a similar transcript was the basis of F.) "I cannot reconcile with any reasonable conception of Shakespeare's methods of work a revision limited to the smoothing out of metre and the substitution of equivalent words, without any incorporation of any new structure or any new ideas. Nor can I think that Shakespeare or anyone else at the theatre would have thought it either worth while or practicable to make actors relearn their parts with an infinity of trivial modifications. Still less can I, with Pollard, suppose that Shakespeare revised the F into the Q form.

"The history of the text must, I think, be somewhat as follows. The play, as written by Shakespeare, was slightly altered for stage purposes. It was shortened by cutting six long passages. Minor alterations were made to enable certain scenes (I. iv., II. i. iv., III. iv. v., V. i. ii. iii.) to be played with a reduced number of minor parts. . . . Q 1 was based on this stage version. I do not think that it was surreptitious, in the sense of being printed without the consent of the Chamberlain's men. There is nothing in the circumstances of the publication to suggest irregularity. Certainly some of the textual features—omissions, paraphrases, substitution of equivalent words, incorporation of actor's 'connectives'—are such as appear in 'reported' plays, and there are some 'auditory' errors. But the text, and in particular the lineation, is so much better than that of the accepted 'bad' quartos, as to suggest the use of a transcript from the original. It must, of course, have been a bad transcript, to explain the verbal divergences from F.[1] I suggest that it was specially prepared by

[1] It is here that I think Sir Edmund Chambers partly begs the question. One might equally justifiably say that F must have been based on a bad transcript, to explain the divergences from Q.

the book-keeper for the printer. . . . His transcription, except for accesses of conscience at III. i. 1 and V. iii. 79, was done carelessly. He was familiar with the play, which he had prompted, and though he generally checked the succession of lines, in writing them out he often allowed himself to follow their purport as he had heard them, thus vulgarising the style, and producing in a minor degree the features of a reported text."

At all events the practical problem for the purposes of this edition was what kind of text to produce; and the Editor confesses that there were moments when the temptation was strong to throw his principles for this occasion to the winds, and produce a conflation, since he feels that whereas F almost certainly represents the original substance of the play (Q cutting speeches and suppressing actors in the interests of brevity and economy), Q probably represents more closely Shakespeare's actual language. On this view Q gives us at any rate nothing but Shakespeare, though far from the whole Shakespeare; F gives us a good deal in addition that is Shakespeare, but also a good deal which quite probably is not. The text here given is therefore verbally that of Q 1. All the passages peculiar to F are inserted in brace brackets { }, those peculiar to Q being indicated by square brackets [ ]. To illustrate one type of divergence a few passages which occur in substantially the same form in the two texts are indicated in the same way, but it is impossible to indicate them all without being vexatious to the reader. At the beginning of the Notes are given three typical passages in full as they appear in the two texts, so that readers can see the kind of problem that is presented and draw their own conclusions. And some of the more significant differences are indicated in the Notes.

DATE OF COMPOSITION. Any external evidence is uncertain and sketchy. The internal evidence of style, as well as the play's obvious connection with *Henry VI*, point to an early date. There is general agreement that it is as early as 1594, and Sir Edmund Chambers would put it a year or so earlier.

AUTHORSHIP. Attempts have been made to discover all manner of other 'hands' in the play, Marlowe, Peele, Kyd, and Drayton among them. These attributions all rest upon subjective impression, and for none of them does there appear to be any valid evidence.

SOURCE. The primary source is Sir Thomas More's life of Richard III as incorporated in the Chronicles of Halle and Holinshed. Shakespeare may have taken a hint or two from *The True Tragedy of Richard III* and from *A Mirror for Magistrates*.

DURATION OF ACTION. The historic time is from 1471 to 1485. The dramatic time is about one month, with eleven days represented on the stage.

CRITICISM. The play is undoubtedly 'powerful,' but with that rather mechanical power of which we are aware in *Titus Andronicus*; one feels that the characters are there for the sake of the play rather than as human beings. Queen Margaret, for example, is no more than an embodied curse, and even Richard himself, dominating figure though he is, and terrible, has something of the abstractness of Tamburlaine.

Hazlitt.—Richard III may be considered as properly a stage-play: it belongs to the theatre rather than to the closet. . . . The Richard of Shakespear is towering and lofty; equally impetuous and commanding; haughty, violent, and subtle; bold and treacherous; confident in his strength as well as in his cunning; raised high by his birth, and higher by his talents and his crimes; a royal usurper, a princely hypocrite, a tyrant and a murderer of the house of Plantagenet. . . . The restless and sanguinary Richard is not a man striving to be great, but to be greater than he is; conscious of his strength of will, his power of intellect, his daring courage, his elevated station; and making use of these advantages to commit unheard-of crimes, and to shield himself from remorse and infamy.

Swinburne.—This only of all Shakespeare's plays belongs absolutely to the school of Marlowe. The influence of the elder master, and that influence alone, is perceptible from end to end. Here at last we can see that Shakespeare has decidedly chosen his side. It is as fiery in passion, as single in purpose, as rhetorical often though never so inflated in expression, as *Tamburlaine* itself. It is doubtless a better piece of work than Marlowe ever did. . . . As certain is it that but for him this play could never have been written. At a later date the subject would have been handled otherwise, had the poet chosen to handle it at all; and in his youth he could not have treated it as he has without the guidance and example of Marlowe. Not only are its highest qualities of energy, of exuberance, of pure and lofty style, of sonorous and successive harmonies, the very qualities that never fail to distinguish those first dramatic models which were fashioned by his ardent hand; the strenuous and single-handed grasp of character, the motion and action of combining and contending powers, which here for the first time we find sustained with equal and unfaltering vigour throughout the length of a whole play, we perceive, though imperfectly, in the work of Marlowe before we can trace them even as latent or infant forces in the work of Shakespeare.

THE TRAGEDY OF
KING RICHARD III

DRAMATIS PERSONÆ

KING EDWARD *the Fourth.*

EDWARD, *Prince of Wales, afterwards King Edward V,*
RICHARD, *Duke of York,* } sons to the King.

GEORGE, *Duke of Clarence,*
RICHARD, *Duke of Gloucester, afterwards King Richard III,* } brothers to the King.

A young son of Clarence.

HENRY, *Earl of Richmond, afterwards King Henry VII.*

CARDINAL BOURCHIER, *Archbishop of Canterbury.*

THOMAS ROTHERHAM, *Archbishop of York.*

JOHN MORTON, *Bishop of Ely.*

DUKE OF BUCKINGHAM.   DUKE OF NORFOLK.

EARL RIVERS, *brother to Elizabeth.*

MARQUIS OF DORSET and LORD GREY, *sons to Elizabeth.*

EARL OF OXFORD.   LORD HASTINGS.

LORD STANLEY, called also EARL OF DERBY.

LORD LOVEL.   SIR WILLIAM CATESBY.

SIR THOMAS VAUGHAN.   SIR JAMES TYRREL.

SIR RICHARD RATCLIFF.   SIR WALTER HERBERT.

SIR ROBERT BRAKENBURY, *Lieutenant of the Tower.*

SIR WILLIAM BRANDON.   CAPTAIN BLUNT.

CHRISTOPHER URSWICK, *a priest.*

TRESSEL and BERKELEY, *gentlemen attending on the Lady Anne.*

Lord Mayor of London.

ELIZABETH, *queen to King Edward IV.*

MARGARET, *widow of King Henry VI.*

DUCHESS OF YORK, *mother to King Edward IV.*

LADY ANNE, *widow of Edward Prince of Wales, son to King Henry VI; afterwards married to Richard.*

A young daughter of Clarence (MARGARET PLANTAGENET).

Ghosts of those murdered by Richard III, Lords and other Attendants, a Priest, a Pursuivant, Scrivener, Citizens, Murderers, Messengers, Soldiers, &c.

SCENE: *England.*

THE TRAGEDY OF KING RICHARD III

Act First

SCENE I

London. A street

Enter Richard, Duke of Gloucester, solus

Gloucester. Now is the winter of our discontent
    Made glorious summer by this sun of York;
    And all the clouds that lour'd upon our house
    In the deep bosom of the ocean buried.
    Now are our brows bound with victorious wreaths,
    Our bruised arms hung up for monuments,
    Our stern alarums chang'd to merry meetings,
    Our dreadful marches to delightful measures.
    Grim-visag'd war hath smooth'd his wrinkled front,
    And now instead of mounting barbed steeds,   10
    To fright the souls of fearful adversaries,
    He capers nimbly in a lady's chamber,
    To the lascivious pleasing of a love.   †
    But I, that am not shap'd for sportive tricks,
    Nor made to court an amorous looking-glass,
    I, that am rudely stamp'd, and want love's majesty
    To strut before a wanton ambling nymph;
    I, that am curtail'd of this fair proportion,
    Cheated of feature by dissembling nature,
    Deform'd, unfinish'd, sent before my time   20
    Into this breathing world scarce half made up,
    And that so lamely and unfashionable,
    That dogs bark at me as I halt by them;
    Why, I, in this weak piping time of peace,
    Have no delight to pass away the time,

Unless to spy my shadow in the sun,
And descant on mine own deformity:
And therefore, since I cannot prove a lover,
To entertain these fair well-spoken days,
I am determined to prove a villain,   30
And hate the idle pleasures of these days.
Plots have I laid, inductions dangerous,
By drunken prophecies, libels and dreams,
To set my brother Clarence and the king
In deadly hate the one against the other.
And if King Edward be as true and just
As I am subtle, false, and treacherous,
This day should Clarence closely be mew'd up,
About a prophecy, which says that G
Of Edward's heirs the murderer shall be.   40
Dive, thoughts, down to my soul: here Clarence comes.

Enter Clarence, guarded, and Brakenbury

Brother, good days: what means this armed guard
  That waits upon your grace?
Clarence.   His majesty,
  Tendering my person's safety, hath appointed
  This conduct to convey me to the Tower.
Gloucester. Upon what cause?
Clarence.   Because my name is George.
Gloucester. Alack, my lord, that fault is none of yours,
  He should for that commit your godfathers:
  O, belike his majesty hath some intent
  That you shall be new-christen'd in the Tower.   50
  But what's the matter, Clarence? may I know?
Clarence. Yea, Richard, when I know; for I protest
  As yet I do not, but, as I can learn,
  He hearkens after prophecies and dreams,
  And from the cross-row plucks the letter G:
  And says a wizard told him that by G
  His issue disinherited should be;
  And for my name of George begins with G,
  It follows in his thought that I am he.
  These, as I learn, and such like toys as these,   60

2

Have mov'd his highness to commit me now.

Gloucester. Why, this it is, when men are rul'd by women;
'Tis not the king that sends you to the Tower,
My Lady Grey his wife, Clarence, 'tis she,
That tempers him to this extremity.   †
Was it not she and that good man of worship,
Anthony Woodville, her brother there,
That made him send Lord Hastings to the Tower,
From whence this present day he is deliver'd?
We are not safe, Clarence, we are not safe.   70

Clarence. By heaven, I think there's no man is secure,
But the queen's kindred, and night-walking heralds,
That trudge betwixt the king and Mistress Shore;   †
Heard ye not what an humble suppliant
Lord Hastings was to her for his delivery?

Gloucester. Humbly complaining to her deity
Got my Lord Chamberlain his liberty.
I'll tell you what, I think it is our way,
If we will keep in favour with the king,
To be her men and wear her livery: 80
The jealous o'erworn widow and herself,
Since that our brother dubb'd them gentlewomen,
Are mighty gossips in this monarchy.

Brakenbury. I beseech your graces both to pardon me;
His majesty hath straitly given in charge
That no man shall have private conference,
Of what degree soever, with his brother.

Gloucester. Even so an 't please your worship, Brakenbury,
You may partake of any thing we say:
We speak no treason, man, we say the king   90
Is wise and virtuous, and his noble queen
Well struck in years, fair, and not jealous;
We say that Shore's wife hath a pretty foot,
A cherry lip, a bonny eye, a passing pleasing tongue;
And that the queen's kindred are made gentle-folks:
How say you, sir? can you deny all this?

Brakenbury. With this, my lord, myself have nought to do.

Gloucester. Naught to do with Mistress Shore! I tell thee,
    fellow,

3

He that doth naught with her, excepting one,
Were best he do it secretly alone.   100
{*Brakenbury.* What one, my lord?
Gloucester. Her husband, knave: wouldst thou betray me?}
Brakenbury. I beseech your grace to pardon me, and withal
  Forbear your conference with the noble duke.
Clarence. We know thy charge, Brakenbury, and will obey.
Gloucester. We are the queen's abjects, and must obey.
  Brother, farewell, I will unto the king,
  And whatsoever you will employ me in,
  Were it to call King Edward's widow sister,
  I will perform it to enfranchise you;   110
  Meantime, this deep disgrace in brotherhood
  Touches me deeper than you can imagine.
Clarence. I know it pleaseth neither of us well.
Gloucester. Well, your imprisonment shall not be long,
  I will deliver you, or {else} lie for you;
  Meantime, have patience.
Clarence.   I must perforce; farewell.
              Exeunt Clarence, Brakenbury, and Guard
Gloucester. Go tread the path that thou shalt ne'er return,
  Simple, plain Clarence, I do love thee so,
  That I will shortly send thy soul to heaven,
  If heaven will take the present at our hands;   120
  But who comes here? the new-deliver'd Hastings?

                        Enter Lord Hastings

Hastings. Good time of day unto my gracious lord!
Gloucester. As much unto my good Lord Chamberlain!
  Well are you welcome to the open air;
  How hath your lordship brook'd imprisonment?
Hastings. With patience, noble lord, as prisoners must:
  But I shall live, my lord, to give them thanks
  That were the cause of my imprisonment.
Gloucester. No doubt, no doubt, and so shall Clarence too,
  For they that were your enemies are his,   130
  And have prevail'd as much on him as you.
Hastings. More pity that the eagle should be mew'd,
  While kites and buzzards prey at liberty.

                              4

Gloucester. What news abroad?

Hastings. No news so bad abroad as this at home;
  The king is sickly, weak and melancholy,
  And his physicians fear him mightily.

Gloucester. Now, by Saint Paul, this news is bad indeed;
  O, he hath kept an evil diet long,
  And overmuch consum'd his royal person;   140
  'Tis very grievous to be thought upon:
  What, is he in his bed?

Hastings. He is.

Gloucester. Go you before, and I will follow you.

                                        Exit Hastings

  He cannot live, I hope, and must not die,
  Till George be pack'd with post-horse up to heaven.
  I'll in, to urge his hatred more to Clarence,
  With lies well steel'd with weighty arguments,
  And if I fail not in my deep intent,
  Clarence hath not another day to live: 150
  Which done, God take King Edward to his mercy,
  And leave the world for me to bustle in;
  For then I'll marry Warwick's youngest daughter.
  What though I kill'd her husband and her father?
  The readiest way to make the wench amends
  Is to become her husband and her father:
  The which will I, not all so much for love,
  As for another secret close intent,
  By marrying her which I must reach unto.
  But yet I run before my horse to market: 160
  Clarence still breathes, Edward still lives and reigns:
  When they are gone, then must I count my gains.   *Exit*

SCENE II

The same. Another street

*Enter the hearse of King Henry the Sixth, Gentlemen with
halberds to guard it; Lady Anne being the mourner*

Lady Anne. Set down, set down your honourable load
  (If honour may be shrouded in a hearse)

5

Whilst I awhile obsequiously lament
The untimely fall of virtuous Lancaster.
Poor key-cold figure of a holy king,
Pale ashes of the house of Lancaster,
Thou bloodless remnant of that royal blood!
Be it lawful that I invocate thy ghost,
To hear the lamentations of poor Anne,
Wife to thy Edward, to thy slaughter'd son,   10
Stabb'd by the selfsame hand that made these holes.
Lo, in these windows that let forth thy life
I pour the helpless balm of my poor eyes;
Curs'd be the hand that made these fatal holes,
Curs'd be the heart that had the heart to do it!
{Cursed the blood that let this blood from hence!}
More direful hap betide that hated wretch,
That makes us wretched by the death of thee,
Than I can wish to adders, spiders, toads,   †
Or any creeping venom'd thing that lives!   20
If ever he have child, abortive be it,
Prodigious and untimely brought to light,
Whose ugly and unnatural aspect
May fright the hopeful mother at the view;
{And that be heir to his unhappiness!}
If ever he have wife, let her be made
As miserable by the death of him,
As I am made by my poor lord and thee!
Come now towards Chertsey with your holy load,
Taken from Paul's to be interred there;   30
And still, as you are weary of the weight,
Rest you, whiles I lament King Henry's corse.

Enter Gloucester

Gloucester. Stay, you that bear the corse, and set it down.
Lady Anne. What black magician conjures up this fiend,
 To stop devoted charitable deeds?
Gloucester. Villains, set down the corse, or, by Saint Paul,
 I'll make a corse of him that disobeys.   †
Gentleman. My lord, stand back, and let the coffin pass.

6

Gloucester. Unmanner'd dog, stand thou, when I com-
   mand:
   Advance thy halberd higher than my breast,   40
   Or, by Saint Paul, I'll strike thee to my foot,
   And spurn upon thee, beggar, for thy boldness.
Lady Anne. What, do you tremble? are you all afraid?
   Alas, I blame you not, for you are mortal,
   And mortal eyes cannot endure the devil.
   Avaunt, thou dreadful minister of hell!
   Thou hadst but power over his mortal body,
   His soul thou canst not have; therefore, be gone.
Gloucester. Sweet saint, for charity, be not so curst.
Lady Anne. Foul devil, for God's sake hence, and trouble
   us not;   50
   For thou hast made the happy earth thy hell,
   Fill'd it with cursing cries and deep exclaims.
   If thou delight to view thy heinous deeds,
   Behold this pattern of thy butcheries.
   O, gentlemen, see, see! dead Henry's wounds
   Open their congeal'd mouths and bleed afresh.
   Blush, blush, thou lump of foul deformity,
   For 'tis thy presence that exhales this blood
   From cold and empty veins where no blood dwells;
   Thy deed, inhuman and unnatural,   60
   Provokes this deluge most unnatural.
   O God, which this blood mad'st, revenge his death,
   O earth, which this blood drink'st, revenge his death!
   Either heaven with lightning strike the murderer dead,
   Or earth, gape open wide and eat him quick,
   As thou dost swallow up this good king's blood,
   Which his hell-govern'd arm hath butchered!
Gloucester. Lady, you know no rules of charity,
   Which renders good for bad, blessings for curses.
Lady Anne. Villain, thou know'st no law of God nor man: 70
   No beast so fierce but knows some touch of pity.
Gloucester. But I know none, and therefore am no beast.
Lady Anne. O wonderful, when devils tell the truth!
Gloucester. More wonderful, when angels are so angry.
   Vouchsafe, divine perfection of a woman,

7

Of these supposed evils to give me leave,
By circumstance but to acquit myself.
Lady Anne. Vouchsafe, defus'd infection of a man,
For these known evils but to give me leave,
By circumstance to curse thy cursed self.   80
Gloucester. Fairer than tongue can name thee, let me have
Some patient leisure to excuse myself.
Lady Anne. Fouler than heart can think thee, thou canst make
No excuse current, but to hang thyself.
Gloucester. By such despair I should accuse myself.
Lady Anne. And by despairing shouldst thou stand excus'd
For doing worthy vengeance on thyself,
Which didst unworthy slaughter upon others.
Gloucester. Say that I slew them not.
Lady Anne.   Why then they are not dead,   †
But dead they are, and, devilish slave, by thee.   90
Gloucester. I did not kill your husband.
Lady Anne.   Why then he is alive.
Gloucester. Nay, he is dead, and slain by Edward's hand.
Lady Anne. In thy foul throat thou liest: Queen Margaret saw
Thy bloody falchion smoking in his blood,   †
The which thou once didst bend against her breast,
But that thy brothers beat aside the point.
Gloucester. I was provoked by her slanderous tongue,
Which laid their guilt upon my guiltless shoulders.
Lady Anne. Thou wast provoked by thy bloody mind,
Which never dreamt on aught but butcheries: 100
Didst thou not kill this king?
Gloucester.   I grant ye.
Lady Anne. Dost grant me, hedgehog? then, God grant me too
Thou mayst be damned for that wicked deed!
O, he was gentle, mild, and virtuous!
Gloucester. The fitter for the King of heaven that hath him.
Lady Anne. He is in heaven, where thou shalt never come.
Gloucester. Let him thank me, that holp to send him thither,

8

For he was fitter for that place than earth.

Lady Anne. And thou unfit for any place but hell.

Gloucester. Yes, one place else, if you will hear me name it. 110

Lady Anne. Some dungeon.

Gloucester.   Your bed-chamber.

Lady Anne. Ill rest betide the chamber where thou liest!

Gloucester. So will it, madam, till I lie with you.

Lady Anne. I hope so.

Gloucester.   I know so. But, gentle Lady Anne,
    To leave this keen encounter of our wits,
    And fall somewhat into a slower method;
    Is not the causer of the timeless deaths
    Of these Plantagenets, Henry and Edward,
    As blameful as the executioner?

Lady Anne. Thou art the cause, and most accurs'd effect. 120

Gloucester. Your beauty was the cause of that effect,
    Your beauty, which did haunt me in my sleep
    To undertake the death of all the world,
    So I might rest one hour in your sweet bosom.   †

Lady Anne. If I thought that, I tell thee, homicide,
    These nails should rend that beauty from my cheeks.

Gloucester. These eyes could never endure sweet beauty's
        wreck,
    You should not blemish them, if I stood by:
    As all the world is cheered by the sun,
    So I by that; it is my day, my life.   130

Lady Anne. Black night o'ershade thy day, and death thy
        life!

Gloucester. Curse not thyself, fair creature, thou art both.

Lady Anne. I would I were, to be reveng'd on thee.

Gloucester. It is a quarrel most unnatural,
    To be reveng'd on him that loveth you.

Lady Anne. It is a quarrel just and reasonable,
    To be reveng'd on him that slew my husband.

Gloucester. He that bereft thee, lady, of thy husband,
    Did it to help thee to a better husband.

Lady Anne. His better doth not breathe upon the earth. 140

Gloucester. [Go to,]
    He lives that loves you better than he could.

9

Lady Anne. Name him.

Gloucester.   Plantagenet.

Lady Anne.   Why, that was he.

Gloucester. The selfsame name, but one of better nature.

Lady Anne. Where is he?

Gloucester.   Here. (*She spitteth at him.*) Why
    dost thou spit at me?

Lady Anne. Would it were mortal poison, for thy sake!

Gloucester. Never came poison from so sweet a place.

Lady Anne. Never hung poison on a fouler toad.
    Out of my sight! thou dost infect my eyes.

Gloucester. Thine eyes, sweet lady, have infected mine.   150

Lady Anne. Would they were basilisks, to strike thee dead!

Gloucester. I would they were, that I might die at once,
    For now they kill me with a living death.
    Those eyes of thine from mine have drawn salt tears,
    Sham'd their aspect with store of childish drops:
    {These eyes, which never shed remorseful tear,
    No, when my father York, and Edward wept,
    To hear the piteous moan that Rutland made
    When black-fac'd Clifford shook his sword at him;
    Nor when thy warlike father, like a child,   160
    Told the sad story of my father's death,
    And twenty times made pause to sob and weep,
    That all the standers-by had wet their cheeks
    Like trees bedash'd with rain: in that sad time
    My manly eyes did scorn an humble tear;
    And what these sorrows could not thence exhale,
    Thy beauty hath, and made them blind with weeping.}
    I never sued to friend nor enemy,
    My tongue could never learn sweet soothing words;
    But, now thy beauty is propos'd my fee,   170
    My proud heart sues, and prompts my tongue to speak.
                            {*She looks scornfully at him*}
    Teach not thy lips such scorn, for they were made
    For kissing, lady, not for such contempt.
    If thy revengeful heart cannot forgive,
    Lo, here I lend thee this sharp-pointed sword;
    Which if thou please to hide in this true bosom,

And let the soul forth that adoreth thee,
I lay it naked to the deadly stroke,
And humbly beg the death upon my knee.
{*He lays his breast open: she offers at it with his sword*}
Nay, do not pause; 'twas I that kill'd your husband,   180
But 'twas thy beauty that provoked me.
Nay, now dispatch; 'twas I that kill'd King Henry,
But 'twas thy heavenly face that set me on.
                            Here she lets fall the sword
Take up the sword again, or take up me.
Lady Anne. Arise, dissembler: though I wish thy death,
    I will not be the executioner.
Gloucester. Then bid me kill myself, and I will do it.
Lady Anne. I have already.
Gloucester.   [Tush,] that was in thy rage:
    Speak it again, and, even with the word,
    That hand, which for thy love did kill thy love,   190
    Shall for thy love kill a far truer love;
    To both their deaths shalt thou be accessary.
Lady Anne. I would I knew thy heart.
Gloucester. 'Tis figur'd in my tongue.
Lady Anne. I fear me both are false.
Gloucester. Then never was man true.
Lady Anne. Well, well, put up your sword.
Gloucester. Say then my peace is made.
Lady Anne. That shall you know hereafter.
Gloucester. But shall I live in hope?   200
Lady Anne. All men, I hope, live so.
Gloucester. Vouchsafe to wear this ring.
Lady Anne. To take is not to give.
Gloucester. Look how this ring encompasseth thy finger,
    Even so thy breast encloseth my poor heart;
    Wear both of them, for both of them are thine,
    And if thy poor devoted suppliant may
    But beg one favour at thy gracious hand
    Thou dost confirm his happiness for ever.
Lady Anne. What is it?   210
Gloucester. That it would please thee leave these sad de-
    signs

11

To him that hath more cause to be a mourner,
And presently repair to Crosby Place,
Where, after I have solemnly interr'd
At Chertsey monastery this noble king,
And wet his grave with my repentant tears,
I will with all expedient duty see you:
For divers unknown reasons, I beseech you,
Grant me this boon.

Lady Anne. With all my heart, and much it joys me too,   220
To see you are become so penitent.
Tressel and Berkeley, go along with me.

Gloucester. Bid me farewell.

Lady Anne.   'Tis more than you deserve;
But since you teach me how to flatter you,
Imagine I have said farewell already.

> *Exeunt Lady Anne, Tressel, and Berkeley*

[*Gloucester.* Sirs, take up the corse.]   †

Gentleman.   Towards Chertsey, noble lord?

Gloucester. No, to White-Friars; there attend my coming.

> *Exeunt all but Gloucester*

Was ever woman in this humour woo'd,
Was ever woman in this humour won?
I'll have her, but I will not keep her long.   230
What? I, that kill'd her husband and his father,
To take her in her heart's extremest hate,
With curses in her mouth, tears in her eyes,
The bleeding witness of her hatred by,
Having God, her conscience, and these bars against me,
And I nothing to back my suit at all,
But the plain devil and dissembling looks,
And yet to win her, all the world to nothing!
Ha!
Hath she forgot already that brave prince,   240
Edward, her lord, whom I, some three months since,
Stabb'd in my angry mood at Tewkesbury?
A sweeter and a lovelier gentleman,
Fram'd in the prodigality of nature,
Young, valiant, wise, and, no doubt, right royal,

The spacious world cannot again afford:
And will she yet debase her eyes on me,
That cropp'd the golden prime of this sweet prince,
And made her widow to a woful bed,
On me, whose all not equals Edward's moiety,   250
On me, that halt, and am unshapen thus?
My dukedom to a beggarly denier,
I do mistake my person all this while;
Upon my life, she finds, although I cannot,
Myself to be a marvellous proper man.
I'll be at charges for a looking-glass,
And entertain some score or two of tailors,
To study fashions to adorn my body,
Since I am crept in favour with myself,
I will maintain it with some little cost: 260
But first I'll turn yon fellow in his grave;
And then return lamenting to my love.
Shine out, fair sun, till I have bought a glass,
That I may see my shadow as I pass.   *Exit*

SCENE III

The palace

Enter Queen Elizabeth, Lord Rivers, and Lord Grey

Rivers. Have patience, madam, there's no doubt his majesty
   Will soon recover his accustom'd health.
Grey. In that you brook it ill, it makes him worse,
   Therefore, for God's sake, entertain good comfort,
   And cheer his grace with quick and merry words.
Queen Eliz. If he were dead, what would betide of me?
Rivers. No other harm but loss of such a lord.
Queen Eliz. The loss of such a lord includes all harm.
Grey. The heavens have bless'd you with a goodly son,
   To be your comforter when he is gone.   10
Queen Eliz. Oh, he is young, and his minority
   Is put unto the trust of Richard Gloucester,
   A man that loves not me nor none of you.
Rivers. Is it concluded he shall be protector?

13

Queen Eliz. It is determin'd, not concluded yet,
But so it must be, if the king miscarry.

Enter Buckingham and Derby

Grey. Here come the lords of Buckingham and Derby.
Buckingham. Good time of day unto your royal grace!
Derby. God make your majesty joyful as you have been!
Queen Eliz. The Countess Richmond, good my Lord of
    Derby,   20
    To your good prayers will scarcely say amen.
    Yet, Derby, notwithstanding she's your wife,
    And loves not me, be you, good lord, assur'd
    I hate not you for her proud arrogance.
Derby. I do beseech you either not believe
    The envious slanders of her false accusers,
    Or, if she be accus'd in true report,
    Bear with her weakness, which, I think, proceeds
    From wayward sickness, and no grounded malice.
Rivers. Saw you the king to-day, my Lord of Derby?   30
Derby. But now the Duke of Buckingham and I
    Came from visiting his majesty.
Queen Eliz. With likelihood of his amendment, lords?
Buckingham. Madam, good hope; his grace speaks cheer-
    fully.
Queen Eliz. God grant him health! Did you confer with
    him?
Buckingham. Madam, we did: he desires to make atonement
    Betwixt the Duke of Gloucester and your brothers,
    And betwixt them and my Lord Chamberlain,
    And sent to warn them to his royal presence.
Queen Eliz. Would all were well! but that will never be: 40
    I fear our happiness is at the highest.

Enter Gloucester, Hastings, and Dorset   †

Gloucester. They do me wrong, and I will not endure it;
    Who are they that complains unto the king,
    That I, forsooth, am sterm and love them not?
    By holy Paul, they love his grace but lightly,
    That fill his ears with such dissentious rumours.

Because I cannot flatter and speak fair,
Smile in men's faces, smooth, deceive and cog,
Duck with French nods and apish courtesy,
I must be held a rancorous enemy.   50
Cannot a plain man live and think no harm,
But thus his simple truth must be abus'd
By silken, sly, insinuating Jacks?
Rivers. To whom in all this presence speaks your grace?
Gloucester. To thee, that hast nor honesty nor grace;
  When have I injur'd thee, when done thee wrong,
  Or thee, or thee, or any of your faction?
  A plague upon you all! His royal person—
  Whom God preserve better than you would wish!—
  Cannot be quiet scarce a breathing-while,   60
  But you must trouble him with lewd complaints.   †
Queen Eliz. Brother of Gloucester, you mistake the matter:
  The king, of his own royal disposition,
  And not provok'd by any suitor else,
  Aiming, belike, at your interior hatred,
  Which in your outward actions shows itself
  Against my kindred, brothers, and myself,
  Makes him to send, that thereby he may gather   †
  The ground of your ill-will, and to remove it.
Gloucester. I cannot tell, the world is grown so bad,   70
  That wrens make prey where eagles dare not perch;
  Since every Jack became a gentleman,
  There's many a gentle person made a Jack.
Queen Eliz. Come, come, we know your meaning, brother
    Gloucester;
  You envy my advancement and my friends':
  God grant we never may have need of you!
Gloucester. Meantime, God grants that we have need of
    you;
  Our brother is imprison'd by your means,
  Myself disgrac'd, and the nobility
  Held in contempt, whilst many fair promotions   80
  Are daily given to ennoble those
  That scarce some two days since were worth a noble.
Queen Eliz. By Him that rais'd me to this careful height,

15

From that contented hap which I enjoy'd,
I never did incense his majesty
Against the Duke of Clarence, but have been
An earnest advocate to plead for him.
My lord, you do me shameful injury,
Falsely to draw me in these vile suspects.

Gloucester. You may deny that you were not the cause   90
Of my Lord Hastings' late imprisonment.

Rivers. She may, my lord, {for}—

Gloucester. She may, Lord Rivers, why, who knows not so?
She may do more, sir, than denying that:
She may help you to many fair preferments,
And then deny her aiding hand therein,
And lay those honours on your high deserts;
What, may she not? She may, yea, marry, may she,—

Rivers. What, marry, may she?

Gloucester. What, marry, may she! marry with a king,   100
A bachelor, a handsome stripling too:
I wis your grandam had a worser match.

Queen Eliz. My Lord of Gloucester, I have too long borne
Your blunt upbraidings and your bitter scoffs:
By heaven, I will acquaint his majesty
With those gross taunts I often have endur'd.
I had rather be a country servant-maid
Than a great queen with this condition,
To be thus taunted, scorn'd, and baited at:

Enter Queen Margaret, behind

Small joy have I in being England's queen.   110

Queen Mar. And lessen'd be that small, God, I beseech thee!
Thy honour, state, and seat is due to me.

Gloucester. What? threat you me with telling of the king?
[Tell him, and spare not: look, what I have said]
I will avouch in presence of the king:
I dare adventure to be sent to the Tower.
'Tis time to speak, my pains are quite forgot.

Queen Mar. Out, devil! I remember them too well,
Thou slewest my husband Henry in the Tower,
And Edward, my poor son, at Tewkesbury.   120

16

Gloucester. Ere you were queen, yea, or your husband king,
   I was a pack-horse in his great affairs,
   A weeder out of his proud adversaries,
   A liberal rewarder of his friends:
   To royalise his blood I spilt mine own.   †
Queen Mar. Yea, and much better blood than his or thine.
Gloucester. In all which time you and your husband Grey
   Were factious for the house of Lancaster;
   And, Rivers, so were you; was not your husband
   In Margaret's battle at Saint Alban's slain?   130
   Let me put in your minds, if yours forget,
   What you have been ere now, and what you are;
   Withal, what I have been, and what I am.
Queen Mar. A murderous villain, and so still thou art.
Gloucester. Poor Clarence did forsake his father, Warwick,
   Yea, and forswore himself, (which Jesu pardon!)
Queen Mar. Which God revenge!
Gloucester. To fight on Edward's party for the crown,
   And for his meed, poor lord, he is mew'd up:
   I would to God my heart were flint, like Edward's.   140
   Or Edward's soft and pitiful, like mine:
   I am too childish-foolish for this world.
Queen Mar. Hie thee to hell for shame, and leave the
     world;
   Thou cacodemon, there thy kingdom is.
Rivers. My Lord of Gloucester, in those busy days,
   Which here you urge to prove us enemies,
   We follow'd then our lord, our lawful king,
   So should we you, if you should be our king.
Gloucester. If I should be? I had rather be a pedlar:
   Far be it from my heart, the thought of it!   150
Queen Eliz. As little joy, my lord, as you suppose
   You should enjoy, were you this country's king,
   As little joy may you suppose in me,
   That I enjoy, being the queen thereof.
Queen Mar. A little joy enjoys the queen thereof,
   For I am she, and altogether joyless.
   I can no longer hold me patient.   *Advancing*
   Hear me, you wrangling pirates, that fall out

17

In sharing that which you have pill'd from me!
Which of you trembles not that looks on me?   160
If not, that, I being queen, you bow like subjects,
Yet that, by you depos'd, you quake like rebels?
O gentle villain, do not turn away!

Gloucester. Foul wrinkled witch, what mak'st thou in my
    sight?

Queen Mar. But repetition of what thou hast marr'd;
    That will I make before I let thee go.

{*Gloucester.* Wert thou not banished on pain of death?

Queen Mar. I was; but I do find more pain in banishment,
    Than death can yield me here by my abode.}
    A husband and a son thou ow'st to me,   170
    And thou a kingdom, all of you allegiance:
    The sorrow that I have, by right is yours,
    And all the pleasures you usurp are mine.

Gloucester. The curse my noble father laid on thee,
    When thou didst crown his warlike brows with paper,   †
    And with thy scorn drew'st rivers from his eyes,
    And then, to dry them, gav'st the duke a clout,
    Steep'd in the faultless blood of pretty Rutland,—
    His curses, then from bitterness of soul
    Denounc'd against thee, are all fall'n upon thee,   180
    And God, not we, hath plagu'd thy bloody deed.

Queen Eliz. So just is God to right the innocent.

Hastings. O, 'twas the foulest deed to slay that babe,
    And the most merciless, that e'er was heard of!

Rivers. Tyrants themselves wept when it was reported.

Dorset. No man but prophesied revenge for it.

Buckingham. Northumberland, then present, wept to see it.

Queen Mar. What? were you snarling all before I came,
    Ready to catch each other by the throat,
    And turn you all your hatred now on me?   190
    Did York's dread curse prevail so much with heaven,
    That Henry's death, my lovely Edward's death,
    Their kingdom's loss, my woful banishment,
    Could all but answer for that peevish brat?
    Can curses pierce the clouds and enter heaven?
    Why, then, give way, dull clouds, to my quick curses!

If not by war, by surfeit die your king,
As ours by murder, to make him a king!
Edward thy son, which now is Prince of Wales,
For Edward my son, which was Prince of Wales,   200
Die in his youth by like untimely violence!
Thyself a queen, for me that was a queen,
Outlive thy glory, like my wretched self!
Long mayst thou live to wail thy children's loss;
And see another, as I see thee now,
Deck'd in thy rights, as thou art stall'd in mine!
Long die thy happy days before thy death,
And, after many lengthen'd hours of grief,
Die neither mother, wife, nor England's queen!
Rivers and Dorset, you were standers by,   210
And so wast thou, Lord Hastings, when my son
Was stabb'd with bloody daggers: God, I pray him,
That none of you may live your natural age,
But by some unlook'd accident cut off!

Gloucester. Have done thy charm, thou hateful wither'd
     hag!

Queen Mar. And leave out thee? stay, dog, for thou shalt
     hear me.
If heaven have any grievous plague in store,
Exceeding those that I can wish upon thee,
O, let them keep it till thy sins be ripe,
And then hurl down their indignation   220
On thee, the troubler of the poor world's peace!
The worm of conscience still begnaw thy soul!
Thy friends suspect for traitors while thou livest,
And take deep traitors for thy dearest friends!
No sleep close up that deadly eye of thine,
Unless it be whilst some tormenting dream
Affrights thee with a hell of ugly devils!
Thou elvish-mark'd, abortive, rooting hog!
Thou that wast seal'd in thy nativity
The slave of nature, and the son of hell,   230
Thou slander of thy mother's heavy womb,
Thou loathed issue of thy father's loins,
Thou rag of honour, thou detested—

Gloucester. Margaret.

Queen Mar.   Richard!

Gloucester.   Ha!

Queen Mar.   I call thee not.

Gloucester. Then I cry thee mercy, for I had thought
  That thou hadst call'd me all these bitter names.

Queen Mar. Why, so I did, but look'd for no reply.
  O, let me make the period to my curse!

Gloucester. 'Tis done by me, and ends in 'Margaret.'

Queen Eliz. Thus have you breath'd your curse against yourself.   240

Queen Mar. Poor painted queen, vain flourish of my
  fortune!
  Why strew'st thou sugar on that bottled spider,
  Whose deadly web ensnareth thee about?
  Fool, fool! thou whet'st a knife to kill thyself;
  The time will come that thou shalt wish for me,
  To help thee curse that poisonous bunch-back'd toad.

Hastings. False-boding woman, end thy frantic curse,
  Lest to thy harm thou move our patience.

Queen Mar. Foul shame upon you! you have all mov'd
  mine.

Rivers. Were you well serv'd, you would be taught your
  duty.   250

Queen Mar. To serve me well, you all should do me duty,
  Teach me to be your queen, and you my subjects:
  O, serve me well, and teach yourselves that duty!

Dorset. Dispute not with her; she is lunatic.

Queen Mar. Peace, master marquess, you are malapert,
  Your fire-new stamp of honour is scarce current.
  O, that your young nobility could judge
  What 'twere to lose it, and be miserable!
  They that stand high have many blasts to shake them,
  And if they fall, they dash themselves to pieces.   260

Gloucester. Good counsel, marry: learn it, learn it, marquess.

Dorset. It toucheth you, my lord, as much as me.

Gloucester. Yea, and much more: but I was born so high,
  Our aery buildeth in the cedar's top,
  And dallies with the wind, and scorns the sun.   †

Queen Mar. And turns the sun to shade, alas! alas!
  Witness my son, now in the shade of death,
  Whose bright out-shining beams thy cloudy wrath
  Hath in eternal darkness folded up.
  Your aery buildeth in our aery's nest.   270
  O God, that seest it, do not suffer it;
  As it was won with blood, lost be it so!
Buckingham. Have done for shame, if not for charity.
Queen Mar. Urge neither charity nor shame to me;
  Uncharitably with me have you dealt,
  And shamefully by you my hopes are butcher'd;
  My charity is outrage, life my shame,
  And in that shame still live my sorrow's rage!
Buckingham. Have done, {have done.}
Queen Mar. O princely Buckingham, I will kiss thy hand,   280
  In sign of league and amity with thee:
  Now fair befall thee and thy princely house!
  Thy garments are not spotted with our blood,
  Nor thou within the compass of my curse.
Buckingham. Nor no one here, for curses never pass
  The lips of those that breathe them in the air.
Queen Mar. I'll not believe but they ascend the sky,
  And there awake God's gentle sleeping peace.
  O Buckingham, beware of yonder dog;
  Look, when he fawns, he bites, and when he bites,   290
  His venom'd tooth will rankle thee to death: †
  Have not to do with him, beware of him;
  Sin, death, and hell have set their marks on him,
  And all their ministers attend on him.
Gloucester. What doth she say, my Lord of Buckingham?
Buckingham. Nothing that I respect, my gracious lord.
Queen Mar. What, dost thou scorn me for my gentle counsel,
  And soothe the devil that I warn thee from?
  O, but remember this another day,
  When he shall split thy very heart with sorrow,   300
  And say poor Margaret was a prophetess.
  Live each of you the subjects of his hate,
  And he to yours, and all of you to God's!   *Exit*

Hastings. My hair doth stand on end to hear her curses.

Rivers. And so doth mine: I wonder she's at liberty.

Gloucester. I cannot blame her, by God's holy mother,
  She hath had too much wrong; and I repent
  My part thereof that I have done {to her.}

Queen Eliz. I never did her any, to my knowledge.

Gloucester. But you have all the vantage of this wrong.   310
  I was too hot to do somebody good,
  That is too cold in thinking of it now.
  Marry, as for Clarence, he is well repaid,
  He is frank'd up to fatting for his pains:
  God pardon them that are the cause of it!

Rivers. A virtuous and a Christian-like conclusion,
  To pray for them that have done scathe to us.

Gloucester. So do I ever: [*aside*] being well advis'd,
  For had I curs'd now, I had curs'd myself.

Enter Catesby

Catesby. Madam, his majesty doth call for you,   320
  And for your grace, and you, my noble lords.

Queen Eliz. Catesby, we come. Lords, will you go with us?

Rivers. Madam, we will attend your grace.

                    Exeunt all but Gloucester

Gloucester. I do the wrong, and first began to brawl.
  The secret mischiefs that I set abroach
  I lay unto the grievous charge of others:
  Clarence, whom I indeed have laid in darkness,
  I do beweep to many simple gulls,
  Namely, to Hastings, Derby, Buckingham,
  And say it is the queen and her allies   330
  That stir the king against the duke my brother.
  Now, they believe me, and withal whet me
  To be reveng'd on Rivers, Vaughan, Grey:
  But then I sigh, and, with a piece of Scripture,
  Tell them that God bids us do good for evil;
  And thus I clothe my naked villany
  With old odd ends stolen out of holy writ,
  And seem a saint when most I play the devil.

Enter two Murderers

But soft! here come my executioners.
How now, my hardy stout resolved mates?   340
Are you now going to dispatch this deed?
First Mur. We are, my lord, and come to have the warrant,
   That we may be admitted where he is.
Gloucester. [It was] well thought upon; I have it here about
      me.   *Gives the warrant*
   When you have done, repair to Crosby Place;
   But, sirs, be sudden in the execution,
   Withal obdurate, do not hear him plead,
   For Clarence is well-spoken, and perhaps
   May move your hearts to pity, if you mark him.   †
First Mur. Tush!   350
   Fear not, my lord, we will not stand to prate,
   Talkers are no good doers: be assur'd:
   We come to use our hands, and not our tongues.
Gloucester. Your eyes drop millstones, when fools' eyes
     drop tears;
   I like you, lads, about your business {straight.
   Go, go, dispatch.
First Mur. We will, my noble lord.}   *Exeunt*

SCENE IV

London. The Tower

Enter Clarence and [Brakenbury] {Keeper}   †

Brakenbury. Why looks your grace so heavily to-day?
Clarence. O, I have pass'd a miserable night,
   So full of ugly sights, of ghastly dreams,
   That, as I am a Christian faithful man,
   I would not spend another such a night,
   Though 'twere to buy a world of happy days,
   So full of dismal terror was the time.
Brakenbury. What was your dream? I long to hear you tell
   it.
Clarence. Methoughts I was embark'd for Burgundy,   †

23

And in my company my brother Gloucester,   10
Who from my cabin tempted me to walk
Upon the hatches; thence we look'd toward England,
And cited up a thousand fearful times,
During the wars of York and Lancaster,
That had befall'n us. As we pac'd along
Upon the giddy footing of the hatches,
Methought that Gloucester stumbled, and, in stumbling,
Struck me, that thought to stay him, overboard,
Into the tumbling billows of the main.
Lord, Lord! methought, what pain it was to drown,   20
What dreadful noise of waters in my ears,
What ugly sights of death within mine eyes!
Methought I saw a thousand fearful wrecks,
Ten thousand men, that fishes gnaw'd upon,
Wedges of gold, great anchors, heaps of pearl,
Inestimable stones, unvalued jewels,
{All scattered in the bottom of the sea:}
Some lay in dead men's skulls, and in those holes,
Where eyes did once inhabit, there were crept,
As 'twere in scorn of eyes, reflecting gems,   30
Which woo'd the slimy bottom of the deep,
And mock'd the dead bones that lay scatter'd by.
Brakenbury. Had you such leisure in the time of death
  To gaze upon the secrets of the deep?
Clarence. Methought I had; {and often did I strive
  To yield the ghost: but} [for] still the envious flood
  Kept in my soul, and would not let it forth,
  To seek the empty vast and wandering air,   †
  But smothered it within my panting bulk,
  Which almost burst to belch it in the sea.   40
Brakenbury. Awak'd you not with this sore agony?
Clarence. O no, my dream was lengthened after life;
  O, then began the tempest to my soul,
  Who pass'd, methought, the melancholy flood,
  With that grim ferryman, which poets write of,
  Unto the kingdom of perpetual night.
  The first that there did greet my stranger soul,

Was my great father-in-law, renowned Warwick,
Who cried aloud, 'What scourge for perjury
Can this dark monarchy afford false Clarence?' 50
And so he vanish'd: then came wandering by
A shadow like an angel in bright hair,
Dabbled in blood, and he squeak'd out aloud,
'Clarence is come, false, fleeting, perjur'd Clarence,
That stabb'd me in the field by Tewkesbury:
Seize on him, Furies, take him to your torments!'
With that, methoughts, a legion of foul fiends
Environ'd me [about], and howled in mine ears
Such hideous cries, that with the very noise
I trembling wak'd, and for a season after 60
Could not believe but that I was in hell,
Such terrible impression made the dream.
Brakenbury. No marvel, my lord, though it affrighted you:
I promise you, I am afraid to hear you tell it.
Clarence. O Brakenbury, I have done those things,
Which now bear evidence against my soul,
For Edward's sake; and see how he requites me!
{O God! if my deep prayers cannot appease thee,
But thou wilt be aveng'd on my misdeeds,
Yet execute thy wrath in me alone; 70
O, spare my guiltless wife, and my poor children!}
I pray thee, gentle keeper, stay by me,
My soul is heavy, and I fain would sleep.
Brakenbury. I will, my lord: God give your grace good rest!
Clarence sleeps

{*Enter Brakenbury*}

Sorrow breaks seasons and reposing hours,
Makes the night morning, and the noon-tide night.
Princes have but their titles for their glories,
An outward honour for an inward toil;
And, for unfelt imagination,
They often feel a world of restless cares: 80
So that, betwixt their titles and low names, †
There's nothing differs but the outward fame.

Enter the two Murderers

{*First Mur.* Ho! who's here?}

Brakenbury. In God's name what are you, and how came
  you hither?

First Mur. I would speak with Clarence, and I came hither
  on my legs.

Brakenbury. Yea, are you so brief?

Sec. Mur. O sir, it is better to be brief than tedious. Show
  him our commission, talk no more.

Brakenbury reads it

Brakenbury. I am in this commanded to deliver   90
  The noble Duke of Clarence to your hands:
  I will not reason what is meant hereby,
  Because I will be guiltless of the meaning.
  Here are the keys, there sits the duke asleep:
  I'll to his Majesty, and certify his grace
  That thus I have resign'd my charge to you.

First Mur. Do so, it is a point of wisdom{: fare you well}.

Exit Brakenbury

Sec. Mur. What, shall I stab him as he sleeps?

First Mur. No; then he will say 'twas done cowardly, when
  he wakes.   100

Sec. Mur. When he wakes! why, fool, he shall never wake
  till the judgement-day.

First Mur. Why, then he will say we stabb'd him sleeping.

Sec. Mur. The urging of that word 'judgement' hath bred
  a kind of remorse in me.

First Mur. What, art thou afraid?

Sec. Mur. Not to kill him, having a warrant [for it]; but
  to be damn'd for killing him, from which no warrant
  can defend us.

{*First Mur.* I thought thou hadst been resolute.   110

Sec. Mur. So I am, to let him live.}

First Mur. Back to the Duke of Gloucester, tell him so.

Sec. Mur. I pray thee, stay a while, I hope my holy humour   †
  will change, 'twas wont to hold me but while one would
  tell twenty.

First Mur. How dost thou feel thyself now?

Sec. Mur. [Faith,] some certain dregs of conscience are yet
within me.

First Mur. Remember our reward when the deed is done.

Sec. Mur. ['Zounds,] he dies, I had forgot the reward.   120

First Mur. Where is thy conscience now?

Sec. Mur. In the Duke of Gloucester's purse.

First Mur. So when he opens his purse to give us our reward, thy conscience flies out.

Sec. Mur. {'Tis no matter,} Let it go, there's few or none
will entertain it.

First Mur. How if it come to thee again?

Sec. Mur. I'll not meddle with it, it is a dangerous thing,
it makes a man a coward. A man cannot steal, but it
accuseth him; he cannot swear, but it checks him; he can-   130
not lie with his neighbour's wife, but it detects him: it is
a blushing shamefast spirit, that mutinies in a man's
bosom; it fills one full of obstacles: it made me once
restore a purse of gold that I found; it beggars any man
that keeps it: it is turn'd out of all towns and cities for
a dangerous thing, and every man that means to live
well endeavours to trust himself and to live without
it.

First Mur. ['Zounds,] it is even now at my elbow, persuad-
ing me not to kill the duke.   140

Sec. Mur. Take the devil in thy mind, and believe him not,
he would insinuate with thee {but} to make thee sigh.

First Mur. Tut, I am strong in fraud, he cannot prevail with   †
me, [I warrant thee].

Sec. Mur. Spoke like a tall fellow that respects his reputa-
tion.

Come, shall we to this gear?   †

First Mur. Take him over the costard with the hilts of thy
sword, and then we will chop him in the malmsey-butt
in the next room.

Sec. Mur. O excellent device! make a sop of him.   150

First Mur. Hark! he stirs: shall I strike?

Sec. Mur. No, first let's reason with him.

Clarence. Where art thou, keeper? give me a cup of wine.

Sec. Mur. You shall have wine enough, my lord, anon.

27

Clarence. In God's name, what art thou?

Sec. Mur. A man, as you are.

Clarence. But not, as I am, royal.

Sec. Mur. Nor you, as we are, loyal.

Clarence. Thy voice is thunder, but thy looks are humble.

Sec. Mur. My voice is now the king's, my looks mine own.   160

Clarence. How darkly and how deadly dost thou speak!

{Your eyes do menace me: why look you pale?}

Tell me who are you, wherefore come you hither?

Both. To, to, to—

Clarence. To murder me?

Both. Ay, {ay.}

Clarence. You scarcely have the hearts to tell me so,

And therefore cannot have the hearts to do it.

Wherein, my friends, have I offended you?

First Mur. Offended us you have not, but the king.   170

Clarence. I shall be reconcil'd to him again.

Sec. Mur. Never, my lord; therefore prepare to die.

Clarence. Are you call'd forth from out a world of men

To slay the innocent? What is my offence?

Where are the evidence that do accuse me?

What lawful quest have given their verdict up

Unto the frowning judge, or who pronounc'd

The bitter sentence of poor Clarence' death?

Before I be convict by course of law,

To threaten me with death is most unlawful.   180

I charge you, as you hope to have redemption,   †

[By Christ's dear blood shed for our grievous sins,]

That you depart and lay no hands on me,

The deed you undertake is damnable.

First Mur. What we will do, we do upon command.

Sec. Mur. And he that hath commanded is the king.

Clarence. Erroneous vassal! the great King of kings

Hath in the tables of his law commanded

That thou shalt do no murder, and wilt thou then

Spurn at his edict, and fulfil a man's?   190

Take heed, for he holds vengeance in his hands,

To hurl upon their heads that break his law.

Sec. Mur. And that same vengeance doth he throw on thee,
  For false forswearing, and for murder too:
  Thou didst receive the [holy] sacrament,   †
  To fight in quarrel of the house of Lancaster.
First Mur. And, like a traitor to the name of God,
  Didst break that vow, and with thy treacherous blade
  Unrip'dst the bowels of thy sovereign's son.
Sec. Mur. Whom thou wert sworn to cherish and defend.   200
First Mur. How canst thou urge God's dreadful law to us,
  When thou hast broke it in so dear degree?
Clarence. Alas, for whose sake did I that ill deed?
  For Edward, for my brother, for his sake:
  [Why, sirs,]
  He sends ye not to murder me for this,
  For in this sin he is as deep as I:
  If God will be revenged for this deed,
  {O, know you yet, he doth it publicly:}
  Take not the quarrel from his powerful arm,   210
  He needs no indirect nor lawless course
  To cut off those that have offended him.
First Mur. Who made thee then a bloody minister,
  When gallant-springing brave Plantagenet,
  That princely novice, was struck dead by thee?
Clarence. My brother's love, the devil, and my rage.
First Mur. Thy brother's love, the devil, and thy fault,   †
  Have brought us hither now to murder thee.
Clarence. Oh, if you love my brother, hate not me;
  I am his brother, and I love him well.   220
  If you be hir'd for meed, go back again,
  And I will send you to my brother Gloucester,
  Who will reward you better for my life,
  Than Edward will for tidings of my death.
Sec. Mur. You are deceiv'd, your brother Gloucester hates
    you.
Clarence. O, no, he loves me, and he holds me dear,
  Go you to him from me.
Both.   Ay, so we will.
Clarence. Tell him, when that our princely father York
  Bless'd his three sons with his victorious arm,

29

[And charg'd us from his soul to love each other,] 230
He little thought of this divided friendship:
Bid Gloucester think of this, and he will weep.
Both. Ay, millstones, as he lesson'd us to weep.
Clarence. O, do not slander him, for he is kind.
First Mur. Right,
  As snow in harvest. Thou deceiv'st thyself:
  'Tis he hath sent us hither now to slaughter thee. †
Clarence. It cannot be, for when I parted with him,
  He hugg'd me in his arms, and swore with sobs
  That he would labour my delivery. 240
Sec. Mur. Why, so he doth, now he delivers thee,
  From this world's thraldom to the joys of heaven.
First Mur. Make peace with God, for you must die, my lord.
Clarence. Hast thou that holy feeling in thy soul,
  To counsel me to make my peace with God;
  And art thou yet to thy own soul so blind,
  That thou wilt war with God, by murdering me?
  Ah, sirs, consider, he that set you on
  To do this deed, will hate you for this deed.
Sec. Mur. What shall we do?
Clarence.   Relent, and save your souls. †
First Mur. Relent? 'tis cowardly and womanish. 251
Clarence. Not to relent is beastly, savage, devilish.
  {Which of you, if you were a prince's son,
  Being pent from liberty, as I am now,
  If two such murderers as yourselves came to you,
  Would not entreat for life?}
  My friend, I spy some pity in thy looks;
  O, if thine eye be not a flatterer,
  Come thou on my side, and entreat for me,
  {As you would beg, were you in my distress:} 260
  A begging prince what beggar pities not?
{*Sec. Mur.* Look behind you, my lord.}
First Mur. Ay, thus, and thus: (*stabs him*) if this will not †
  serve,
  I'll chop thee in the malmsey-butt, in the next room.
                      Exit, with the body

Sec. Mur. A bloody deed, and desperately perform'd;
    How fain, like Pilate, would I wash my hands
    Of this most grievous [guilty] murder [done]!

Re-enter First Murderer

First Mur. Why dost thou not help me?
    By heavens, the duke shall know how slack thou art!
Sec. Mur. I would he knew that I had sav'd his brother!   270
    Take thou the fee, and tell him what I say,
    For I repent me that the duke is slain.   *Exit*
First Mur. So do not I: go, coward as thou art.
    Now must I hide his body in some hole,
    Until the duke take order for his burial:
    And when I have my meed, I must away,
    For this will out, and here I must not stay.   *Exit*

Act Second

SCENES I AND II

London. The palace

*Flourish. Enter King Edward sick, Queen Elizabeth,
Dorset, Rivers, Hastings, Buckingham, Grey, and others*

King Edward. {Why}, so: now have I done a good day's
    work:
    You peers, continue this united league:
    I every day expect an embassage
    From my Redeemer to redeem me hence;
    And now in peace my soul shall part for heaven,
    Since I have set my friends at peace on earth.
    Rivers and Hastings, take each other's hand,   †
    Dissemble not your hatred, swear your love.
Rivers. By heaven, my heart is purg'd from grudging hate,
    And with my hand I seal my true heart's love.   10
Hastings. So thrive I, as I truly swear the like!

31

King Edward. Take heed you dally not before your king,
    Lest he that is the supreme King of kings
    Confound your hidden falsehood, and award
    Either of you to be the other's end.
Hastings. So prosper I, as I swear perfect love!
Rivers. And I, as I love Hastings with my heart!
King Edward. Madam, yourself are not exempt in this,
    Nor your son Dorset, Buckingham, nor you;
    You have been factious one against the other.   20
    Wife, love Lord Hastings, let him kiss your hand,
    And what you do, do it unfeignedly.
Queen Eliz. Here, Hastings; I will never more remember
    Our former hatred, so thrive I and mine!
{*King Edward.* Dorset, embrace him; Hastings, love lord
    marquess.}
Dorset. This interchange of love, I here protest,
    Upon my part shall be unviolable.
Hastings. And so swear I, [my lord.]   *They embrace*
King Edward. Now, princely Buckingham, seal thou this
    league
    With thy embracements to my wife's allies,   30
    And make me happy in your unity.
Buckingham. (*to the Queen*) Whenever Buckingham doth
    turn his hate
    On you or yours, but with all duteous love
    Doth cherish you and yours, God punish me
    With hate in those where I expect most love!
    When I have most need to employ a friend,
    And most assured that he is a friend,
    Deep, hollow, treacherous and full of guile,
    Be he unto me, this do I beg of God,
    When I am cold in zeal to you or yours.   40
                    They embrace
King Edward. A pleasing cordial, princely Buckingham,
    Is this thy vow unto my sickly heart.
    There wanteth now our brother Gloucester here,
    To make the perfect period of this peace.
Buckingham. And, in good time, here comes the noble duke.   †

Enter Gloucester

Gloucester. Good morrow to my sovereign king and queen,
    And, princely peers, a happy time of day!
King Edward. Happy indeed, as we have spent the day:
    Brother, we have done deeds of charity;
    Made peace of enmity, fair love of hate,   50
    Between these swelling wrong-incensed peers.
Gloucester. A blessed labour, my most sovereign liege:
    Amongst this princely heap, if any here,
    By false intelligence, or wrong surmise,
    Hold me a foe;
    If I unwittingly, or in my rage,
    Have aught committed that is hardly borne
    By any in this presence, I desire
    To reconcile me to his friendly peace:
    'Tis death to me to be at enmity;   60
    I hate it, and desire all good men's love.
    First, madam, I entreat true peace of you,
    Which I will purchase with my duteous service;
    Of you, my noble cousin Buckingham,
    If ever any grudge were lodg'd between us;
    Of you, Lord Rivers, and, Lord Grey, of you,   †
    That all without desert have frown'd on me;
    {Of you, Lord Woodvill, and, Lord Scales, of you}
    Dukes, earls, lords, gentlemen; indeed, of all.
    I do not know that Englishman alive   70
    With whom my soul is any jot at odds,
    More than the infant that is born to-night:
    I thank my God for my humility.
Queen Eliz. A holy day shall this be kept hereafter:
    I would to God all strifes were well compounded.
    My sovereign liege, I do beseech your majesty
    To take our brother Clarence to your grace.
Gloucester. Why, madam, have I offer'd love for this,
    To be so scorned in this royal presence?
    Who knows not that the noble duke is dead?   80
                      {They all start}

    You do him injury to scorn his corse.

Rivers. Who knows not he is dead? who knows he is?
Queen Eliz. All-seeing heaven, what a world is this!
Buckingham. Look I so pale, Lord Dorset, as the rest?
Dorset. Ay, my good lord; and no one in this presence
    But his red colour hath forsook his cheeks.
King Edward. Is Clarence dead? the order was revers'd.
Gloucester. But he, poor soul, by your first order died,
    And that a winged Mercury did bear,
    Some tardy cripple bore the countermand,   90
    That came too lag to see him buried.
    God grant that some, less noble and less loyal,
    Nearer in bloody thoughts, but not in blood,
    Deserve not worse than wretched Clarence did,
    And yet go current from suspicion!

Enter the Earl of Derby

Derby. A boon, my sovereign, for my service done!
King Edward. I pray thee, peace; my soul is full of sorrow.
Derby. I will not rise, unless your highness grant.   †
King Edward. Then speak at once what is it thou demand'st.
Derby. The forfeit, sovereign, of my servant's life,   100
    Who slew to-day a riotous gentleman
    Lately attendant on the Duke of Norfolk.
King Edward. Have I a tongue to doom my brother's death,
    And shall the same give pardon to a slave?
    My brother slew no man, his fault was thought,
    And yet his punishment was cruel death.
    Who sued to me for him? who, in my rage,
    Kneel'd at my feet and bade me be advis'd?
    Who spake of brotherhood? who {spake} of love?
    Who told me how the poor soul did forsake   110
    The mighty Warwick, and did fight for me?
    Who told me, in the field by Tewkesbury,
    When Oxford had me down, he rescued me,
    And said 'Dear brother, live, and be a king'?
    Who told me, when we both lay in the field
    Frozen almost to death, how he did lap me
    Even in his own garments, and gave himself,
    All thin and naked, to the numb cold night?

All this from my remembrance brutish wrath
Sinfully pluck'd, and not a man of you   120
Had so much grace to put it in my mind.
But when your carters, or your waiting-vassals,
Have done a drunken slaughter, and defac'd
The precious image of our dear Redeemer,
You straight are on your knees for pardon, pardon;
And I unjustly too must grant it you:
But for my brother, not a man would speak,
Nor I, ungracious, speak unto myself,
For him, poor soul. The proudest of you all
Have been beholding to him in his life;   130
Yet none of you would once plead for his life.
O God, I fear thy justice will take hold
On me, and you, and mine, and yours for this!
Come, Hastings, help me to my closet. Oh, poor Clarence!
> *Exeunt some with King and Queen*

Gloucester. This is the fruit of rashness. Mark'd you not
How that the guilty kindred of the queen
Look'd pale when they did hear of Clarence' death?
O, they did urge it still unto the king!
God will revenge it. But come, let's in,
To comfort Edward with our company.   140
{*Buckingham.* We wait upon your grace.}   *Exeunt*

*Enter the Duchess of York, with the two children
of Clarence*

Boy. Tell, me, good grandam, is our father dead?
Duchess. No, boy.
Boy. Why do you wring your hands, and beat your breast,
    And cry 'O Clarence, my unhappy son'?
Girl. Why do you look on us, and shake your head,
    And call us wretches, orphans, castaways,
    If that our noble father be alive?
Duchess. My pretty cousins, you mistake me much.

35

I do lament the sickness of the king,
As loath to lose him, not your father's death; 10
It were lost labour to weep for one that's lost.
Boy. Then, grandam, you conclude that he is dead.
The king my uncle is to blame for this:
God will revenge it, whom I will importune
With daily prayers, all to that effect.
{*Girl.* And so will I.}
Duchess. Peace, children, peace! the king doth love you
well:
Incapable and shallow innocents,
You cannot guess who caus'd your father's death.
Boy. Grandam, we can; for my good uncle Gloucester 20
Told me, the king, provoked by the queen,
Devis'd impeachments to imprison him:
And when he told me so, he wept, †
And hugg'd me in his arm, and kindly kiss'd my cheek,
And bade me rely on him as on my father,
And he would love me dearly as his child.
Duchess. Oh, that deceit should steal such gentle shapes,
And with a virtuous vizard hide foul guile!
He is my son, yea, and therein my shame;
Yet from my dugs he drew not this deceit. 30
Boy. Think you my uncle did dissemble, grandam?
Duchess. Ay, boy.
Boy. I cannot think it. Hark! what noise is this?

> Enter Queen Elizabeth, {*with her hair about her ears;* †
> *Rivers and Dorset after her*}

Queen Eliz. Oh, who shall hinder me to wail and weep?
To chide my fortune, and torment myself?
I'll join with black despair against my soul,
And to myself become an enemy.
Duchess. What means this scene of rude impatience?
Queen. Eliz. To make an act of tragic violence:
Edward, my lord, your son, our king, is dead. 40
Why grow the branches, now the root is wither'd?
Why wither not the leaves, the sap being gone?
If you will live, lament; if die, be brief;

That our swift-winged souls may catch the king's,
Or, like obedient subjects, follow him
To his new kingdom of perpetual rest.   †
Duchess. Ah, so much interest have I in thy sorrow
As I had title in thy noble husband!
I have bewept a worthy husband's death,
And liv'd by looking on his images.   50
But now two mirrors of his princely semblance
Are crack'd in pieces by malignant death;
And I for comfort have but one false glass,
Which grieves me when I see my shame in him.
Thou art a widow, yet thou art a mother,
And hast the comfort of thy children left [thee:]
But death hath snatch'd my husband from mine arms,
And pluck'd two crutches from my feeble limbs,
Edward and Clarence; O, what cause have I,
Thine being but a moiety of my grief,   60
To overgo thy plaints and drown thy cries!
Boy. Good aunt, you wept not for our father's death,
How can we aid you with our kindred tears?
Girl. Our fatherless distress was left unmoan'd,
Your widow's dolours likewise be unwept!
Queen Eliz. Give me no help in lamentation,
I am not barren to bring forth laments:
All springs reduce their currents to mine eyes,
That I, being govern'd by the watery moon,
May send forth plenteous tears to drown the world!   70
Oh for my husband, for my dear lord Edward!
Children. Oh for our father, for our dear lord Clarence!
Duchess. Alas for both, both mine, Edward and Clarence!
Queen Eliz. What stay had I but Edward? and he is gone.
Children. What stay had we but Clarence? and he is gone.
Duchess. What stays had I but they? and they are gone.
Queen Eliz. Was never widow had so dear a loss.
Children. Was never orphans had a dearer loss.
Duchess. Was never mother had a dearer loss.
Alas, I am the mother of these moans!   80
Their woes are parcell'd, mine are general.

37

She for an Edward weeps, and so do I;
I for a Clarence weep, so doth not she:
These babes for Clarence weep, [and so do I;
I for an Edward weep,] so do not they:
Alas, you three, on me threefold distress'd
Pour all your tears! I am your sorrow's nurse,
And I will pamper it with lamentations.
{*Dorset.* Comfort, dear mother: God is much displeased
   That you take with unthankfulness his doing: 90
   In common worldly things, 'tis call'd ungrateful,
   With dull unwillingness to repay a debt
   Which with a bounteous hand was kindly lent;
   Much more to be thus opposite with heaven,
   For it requires the royal debt it lent you.
Rivers. Madam, bethink you, like a careful mother,
   Of the young prince your son: send straight for him;
   Let him be crown'd; in him your comfort lives:
   Drown desperate sorrow in dead Edward's grave,
   And plant your joys in living Edward's throne.}   100

      Enter Gloucester, Buckingham, {Derby, Hastings,
                and Ratcliff}

Gloucester. Madam, have comfort: all of us have cause
   To wail the dimming of our shining star;
   But none can cure their harms by wailing them;
   Madam, my mother, I do cry you mercy,
   I did not see your grace; humbly on my knee
   I crave your blessing.
Duchess. God bless thee, and put meekness in thy mind,
   Love, charity, obedience, and true duty!
Gloucester. (*aside*) Amen, and make me die a good old
   man!
   That is the butt-end of a mother's blessing: 110
   I marvel why her grace did leave it out.
Buckingham. You cloudy princes, and heart-sorrowing
   peers,
   That bear this mutual heavy load of moan,
   Now cheer each other in each other's love:

Though we have spent our harvest of this king,
We are to reap the harvest of his son.
The broken rancour of your high-swoln hearts,
But lately splinter'd, knit, and join'd together,
Must gently be preserv'd, cherish'd, and kept:
Me seemeth good that with some little train   120
Forthwith from Ludlow the young prince be fetch'd
Hither to London, to be crown'd our king.
{*Rivers.* Why with some little train, my Lord of Bucking-
ham?
Buckingham. Marry, my lord, lest, by a multitude,
The new-heal'd wound of malice should break out;
Which would be so much the more dangerous,
By how much the estate is green and yet ungovern'd: †
Where every horse bears his commanding rein,
And may direct his course as please himself,
As well the fear of harm as harm apparent,   130
In my opinion, ought to be prevented.
Gloucester. I hope the king made peace with all of us;
And the compact is firm and true in me.
Rivers. And so in me; and so, I think, in all:
Yet, since it is but green, it should be put
To no apparent likelihood of breach,
Which haply by much company might be urg'd:
Therefore I say with noble Buckingham,
That it is meet so few should fetch the prince.
Hastings. And so say I.}   140
Gloucester. Then be it so; and go we to determine
Who they shall be that straight shall post to Ludlow.
Madam, and you my mother, will you go
To give your censures in this [weighty] business?
Queen Eliz.
Duchess. } With all our hearts.
                    Exeunt all but Buckingham and Gloucester
Buckingham. My lord, whoever journeys to the prince,
For God's sake, let not us two stay behind:
For, by the way, I'll sort occasion,
As index to the story we late talk'd of,
To part the queen's proud kindred from the king.   150

Gloucester. My other self, my counsel's consistory,
  My oracle, my prophet, my dear cousin,
  I, like a child, will go by thy direction.
  Towards Ludlow then, for we'll not stay behind.

                                                    Exeunt

SCENE III

London. A street

Enter two Citizens, meeting

First Cit. Neighbour, well met, whither away so fast?
Sec. Cit. I promise you, I scarcely know myself:
First Cit. Hear you the news abroad?
Sec. Cit.   Ay, that the king is dead.
First Cit. Bad news, by 'r lady, seldom comes the better:
  I fear, I fear, 'twill prove a troublous world.

Enter another Citizen

{*Third Cit.* Neighbours, God speed!
First Cit.   Give you good morrow, sir.}
Third Cit. [Good morrow, neighbours]
  Doth this news hold of good King Edward's death?
[*First Cit.* It doth.]
{*Sec. Cit.* Ay, sir, it is too true; God help the while!}   10
Third Cit. Then, masters, look to see a troublous world.
First Cit. No, no; by God's good grace his son shall reign.
Third Cit. Woe to that land that's govern'd by a child!
Sec. Cit. In him there is a hope of government,
  That in his nonage council under him,
  And in his full and ripen'd years himself,
  No doubt, shall then and till then govern well.
First Cit. So stood the state when Harry the Sixth
  Was crown'd in Paris, but at nine months old.
Third Cit. Stood the state so? No, good my friends, not so;   20
  For then this land was famously enrich'd
  With politic grave counsel; then the king
  Had virtuous uncles to protect his grace.

40

Sec. Cit. {Why,} so hath this, both by the father and
    mother.
Third Cit. Better it were they all came by the father,
    Or by the father there were none at all;
    For emulation now, who shall be nearest,
    Will touch us all too near, if God prevent not.
    O, full of danger is the Duke of Gloucester,
    And the queen's kindred haughty and proud,   †
    And were they to be rul'd, and not to rule,   31
    This sickly land might solace as before.
Sec. Cit. Come, come, we fear the worst, all shall be well.
Third Cit. When clouds appear, wise men put on their
    cloaks;
    When great leaves fall, the winter is at hand;
    When the sun sets, who doth not look for night?
    Untimely storms make men expect a dearth.
    All may be well; but, if God sort it so,
    'Tis more than we deserve, or I expect.
First Cit. Truly, the souls of men are full of dread: †
    Ye cannot almost reason with a man   41
    That looks not heavily, and full of fear.
Third Cit. Before the times of change, still is it so:
    By a divine instinct men's minds mistrust
    Ensuing dangers, as, by proof, we see
    The waters swell before a boisterous storm.
    But leave it all to God. Whither away?
Sec. Cit. {Marry,} we are sent for to the justices.
Third Cit. And so was I: I'll bear you company.   *Exeunt*

SCENE IV

London. The palace

Enter the [Cardinal] {Archbishop}, the young Duke of   †
York, Queen Elizabeth, and the Duchess of York

Cardinal. Last night I hear they lay at Northampton,   †
    At Stony-Stratford will they be to-night,
    To-morrow, or next day, they will be here.
Duchess. I long with all my heart to see the prince;

I hope he is much grown since last I saw him.
Queen Eliz. But I hear, no; they say my son of York
    Hath almost overta'en him in his growth.
York. Ay, mother; but I would not have it so.
Duchess. Why, my young cousin, it is good to grow.
York. Grandam, one night as we did sit at supper,   10
    My uncle Rivers talk'd how I did grow
    More than my brother: 'Ay,' quoth my uncle Gloucester,
    'Small herbs have grace, great weeds do grow apace:'
    And since, methinks, I would not grow so fast,
    Because sweet flowers are slow, and weeds make haste.
Duchess. Good faith, good faith, the saying did not hold
    In him that did object the same to thee:
    He was the wretched'st thing when he was young,
    So long a-growing and so leisurely,
    That, if this rule were true, he should be gracious.   20
Cardinal. Why, madam, so no doubt he is.
Duchess. I hope so too, but yet let mothers doubt.
York. Now, by my troth, if I had been remember'd,
    I could have given my uncle's grace a flout,
    That should have nearer touch'd his growth than he did
      mine.   †
Duchess. How, my pretty York? I pray thee, let me hear it.
York. Marry, they say my uncle grew so fast
    That he could gnaw a crust at two hours old:
    'Twas full two years ere I could get a tooth.
    Grandam, this would have been a biting jest.   30
Duchess. I pray thee, pretty York, who told thee so?
York. Grandam, his nurse.
Duchess. His nurse? why, she was dead ere thou wert born.
York. If 'twere not she, I cannot tell who told me.
Queen Eliz. A parlous boy: go to, you are too shrewd.
Cardinal. Good madam, be not angry with the child.
Queen Eliz. Pitchers have ears.

Enter Dorset   †

Cardinal. Here comes your son, Lord Marquess Dorset;
    What news, Lord Marquess?
Dorset. Such news, my lord, as grieves me to unfold.   40

Queen Eliz. How fares the prince?
Dorset.   Well, madam, and in health.
Duchess. What is thy news [then?]
Dorset. Lord Rivers and Lord Grey are sent to Pomfret,
  With them Sir Thomas Vaughan, prisoners.
Duchess. Who hath committed them?
Dorset.   The mighty dukes,
  Gloucester and Buckingham.
Cardinal.   For what offence?
Dorset. The sum of all I can, I have disclos'd;
  Why, or for what, these nobles were committed
  Is all unknown to me, my gracious lady,
Queen Eliz. Ay me, I see the downfall of our house;   50
  The tiger now hath seiz'd the gentle hind;
  Insulting tyranny begins to jet
  Upon the innocent and lawless throne: †
  Welcome, destruction, death, and massacre!
  I see, as in a map, the end of all.
Duchess. Accursed and unquiet wrangling days,
  How many of you have mine eyes beheld!
  My husband lost his life to get the crown;
  And often up and down my sons were toss'd,
  For me to joy and weep their gain and loss: 60
  And being seated, and domestic broils
  Clean over-blown, themselves, the conquerors,
  Make war upon themselves, blood against blood,
  Self against self: O, preposterous
  And frantic outrage, end thy damned spleen;
  Or let me die, to look on death no more!
Queen Eliz. Come, come, my boy, we will to sanctuary.
  {Madam, farewell.}
Duchess.   I'll go along with you.
Queen Eliz. You have no cause.
Cardinal   My gracious lady, go,
  And thither bear your treasure and your goods;   70
  For my part, I'll resign unto your grace
  The seal I keep, and so betide to me,
  As well I tender you and all of yours!
  Come, I'll conduct you to the sanctuary.   *Exeunt*

Act Third

London. A street

The trumpets sound. Enter the young Prince, the Dukes of Gloucester and Buckingham, Cardinal Bourchier, Catesby, and others

Buckingham. Welcome, sweet prince, to London, to your
    chamber.
Gloucester. Welcome, dear cousin, my thoughts' sovereign;
    The weary way hath made you melancholy.
Prince. No, uncle, but our crosses on the way
    Have made it tedious, wearisome, and heavy:
    I want more uncles here to welcome me.
Gloucester. Sweet prince, the untainted virtue of your
    years
    Hath not yet div'd into the world's deceit:
    Nor more can you distinguish of a man
    Than of his outward show, which, God he knows,   10
    Seldom or never jumpeth with the heart.
    Those uncles which you want were dangerous;
    Your grace attended to their sugar'd words,
    But look'd not on the poison of their hearts:
    God keep you from them, and from such false friends!
Prince. God keep me from false friends! but they were
    none.
Gloucester. My lord, the mayor of London comes to greet
    you.

Enter the Lord Mayor, and his train

Lord Mayor. God bless your grace with health and happy
    days!
Prince. I thank you, good my lord; and thank you all.
    I thought my mother, and my brother York,   20

44

Would long ere this have met us on the way:
Fie, what a slug is Hastings, that he comes not
To tell us whether they will come or no!

Enter Lord Hastings

Buckingham. And, in good time, here comes the sweating
    lord.
Prince. Welcome, my lord: what, will our mother come?
Hastings. On what occasion, God he knows, not I,
    The queen your mother and your brother York
    Have taken sanctuary: the tender prince
    Would fain have come with me to meet your grace,
    But by his mother was perforce withheld.   30
Buckingham. Fie, what an indirect and peevish course
    Is this of hers! Lord cardinal, will your grace
    Persuade the queen to send the Duke of York
    Unto his princely brother presently
    If she deny, Lord Hastings, go with him,
    And from her jealous arms pluck him perforce.
Cardinal. My Lord of Buckingham, if my weak oratory
    Can from his mother win the Duke of York,
    Anon expect him here; but if she be obdurate
    To mild entreaties, God [in heaven] forbid   40
    We should infringe the holy privilege
    Of blessed sanctuary! not for all this land
    Would I be guilty of so deep a sin.
Buckingham. You are too senseless-obstinate, my lord,
    Too ceremonious and traditional:
    Weigh it but with the grossness of this age,
    You break not sanctuary in seizing him.
    The benefit thereof is always granted
    To those whose dealings have deserv'd the place,
    And those who have the wit to claim the place: 50
    This prince hath neither claim'd it nor deserv'd it,
    And therefore, in mine opinion, cannot have it:
    Then, taking him from thence that is not there,
    You break no privilege nor charter there.
    Oft have I heard of sanctuary men,
    But sanctuary children ne'er till now.

Cardinal. My lord, you shall o'er-rule my mind for once.
   Come on, Lord Hastings, will you go with me?
Hastings. I go, my lord.
Prince. Good lords, make all the speedy haste you may.   60
                    Exeunt Cardinal and Hastings
   Say, uncle Gloucester, if our brother come,
   Where shall we sojourn till our coronation?
Gloucester. Where it seems best unto your royal self:
   If I may counsel you, some day or two
   Your highness shall repose you at the Tower:
   Then where you please, and shall be thought most fit
   For your best health and recreation.
Prince. I do not like the Tower, of any place.
   Did Julius Cæsar build that place, my lord?
Buckingham. He did, my gracious lord, begin that place,   70
   Which, since, succeeding ages have re-edified.
Prince. Is it upon record, or else reported
   Successively from age to age, he built it?
Buckingham. Upon record, my gracious lord.
Prince. But say, my lord, it were not register'd,
   Methinks the truth should live from age to age,
   As 'twere retail'd to all posterity,
   Even to the general [all]-ending day.
Gloucester. (*aside*) So wise so young, they say, do ne'er
   live long.
Prince. What say you, uncle?   80
Gloucester. I say, without characters fame lives long.
   (*aside*) Thus, like the formal vice, Iniquity,   †
   I moralize two meanings in one word.
Prince. That Julius Cæsar was a famous man;
   With what his valour did enrich his wit,
   His wit set down to make his valour live:
   Death makes no conquest of this conqueror,
   For now he lives in fame, though not in life.
   I'll tell you what, my cousin Buckingham,—
Buckingham. What, my gracious lord?   90
Prince. An if I live until I be a man,
   I'll win our ancient right in France again,
   Or die a soldier, as I liv'd a king.

Gloucester. (*aside*) Short summers lightly have a forward
   spring.

   Enter young York, Hastings, and the Cardinal

Buckingham. Now, in good time, here comes the Duke of
   York.
Prince. Richard of York! how fares our loving brother?
York. Well, my dread lord; so must I call you now.
Prince. Ay, brother, to our grief, as it is yours:
   Too late he died that might have kept that title,
   Which by his death hath lost much majesty.   100
Gloucester. How fares our cousin, noble Lord of York?
York. I thank you, gentle uncle. O, my lord,
   You said that idle weeds are fast in growth:
   The prince my brother hath outgrown me far.
Gloucester. He hath, my lord.
York.   And therefore is he idle?
Gloucester. O, my fair cousin, I must not say so.
York. Then he is more beholding to you than I.
Gloucester. He may command me as my sovereign,
   But you have power in me as in a kinsman.
York. I pray you, uncle, give me this dagger.   110
Gloucester. My dagger, little cousin? with all my heart.
Prince. A beggar, brother?
York. Of my kind uncle, that I know will give,
   And being but a toy, which is no grief to give.
Gloucester. A greater gift than that I'll give my cousin.
York. A greater gift? O, that's the sword to it.
Gloucester. Ay, gentle cousin, were it light enough.
York. O, then, I see, you'll part but with light gifts;
   In weightier things you'll say a beggar nay.
Gloucester. It is too heavy for your grace to wear.   120
York. I weigh it lightly, were it heavier.
Gloucester. What, would you have my weapon, little lord?
York. I would, that I might thank you as you call me.
Gloucester. How?
York. Little.
Prince. My Lord of York will still be cross in talk:
   Uncle, your grace knows how to bear with him.

47

York. You mean, to bear me, not to bear with me:
   Uncle, my brother mocks both you and me;
   Because that I am little, like an ape,   130
   He thinks that you should bear me on your shoulders.
Buckingham. With what a sharp provided wit he reasons!
   To mitigate the scorn he gives his uncle,
   He prettily and aptly taunts himself:
   So cunning and so young is wonderful.
Gloucester. My lord, will 't please you pass along?
   Myself and my good cousin Buckingham
   Will to your mother, to entreat of her
   To meet you at the Tower, and welcome you.
York. What, will you go unto the Tower, my lord?   140
Prince. My lord protector [needs] will have it so.
York. I shall not sleep in quiet at the Tower.
Gloucester. Why, what should you fear?
York. Marry, my uncle Clarence' angry ghost:
   My grandam told me he was murder'd there.
Prince. I fear no uncles dead.
Gloucester. Nor none that live, I hope.
Prince. An if they live, I hope I need not fear.
   But come, my lord; {and} with a heavy heart,
   Thinking on them, go I unto the Tower.   150
              A Sennet. Exeunt all but Gloucester,
                       Buckingham and Catesby
Buckingham. Think you, my lord, this little prating York
   Was not incensed by his subtle mother
   To taunt and scorn you thus opprobriously?
Gloucester. No doubt, no doubt: O, 'tis a perilous boy,
   Bold, quick, ingenious, forward, capable,
   He is all the mother's, from the top to toe.
Buckingham. Well, let them rest. Come hither, Catesby.
   Thou art sworn as deeply to effect what we intend,
   As closely to conceal what we impart:
   Thou know'st our reasons urg'd upon the way;   160
   What think'st thou? is it not an easy matter
   To make William Lord Hastings of our mind,
   For the instalment of this noble duke
   In the seat royal of this famous isle?

Catesby. He for his father's sake so loves the prince,
  That he will not be won to aught against him.
Buckingham. What think'st thou then of Stanley? what will
    he?
Catesby. He will do all in all as Hastings doth.
Buckingham. Well, then, no more but this:
  Go, gentle Catesby, and, as it were afar off,   170
  Sound thou Lord Hastings, how he stands affected;
  Unto our purpose; [if he be willing]
  {And summon him to-morrow to the Tower,
  To sit about the coronation.
  If thou dost find him tractable to us,}
  Encourage him, and show him all our reasons:
  If he be leaden, icy, cold, unwilling,
  Be thou so too; and so break off your talk,
  And give us notice of his inclination:
  For we to-morrow hold divided councils,   180
  Wherein thyself shalt highly be employ'd.
Gloucester. Commend me to Lord William; tell him,
    Catesby,
  His ancient knot of dangerous adversaries
  To-morrow are let blood at Pomfret Castle,
  And bid my friend, for joy of this good news,
  Give Mistress Shore one gentle kiss the more.
Buckingham. Good Catesby, {go,} effect this business
  soundly.
Catesby. My good lords both, with all the heed I may.
Gloucester. Shall we hear from you, Catesby, ere we sleep?
Catesby. You shall, my lord.   190
Gloucester. At Crosby Place, there shall you find us both.
                      Exit Catesby
Buckingham. Now, my lord, what shall we do, if we per-
  ceive
  [William] Lord Hastings will not yield to our complots?
Gloucester. Chop off his head, [man;] somewhat we will
  do:
  And, look, when I am king, claim thou of me
  The earldom of Hereford, and the moveables
  Whereof the king my brother stood possess'd.

49

Buckingham. I'll claim that promise at your grace's hands.
Gloucester. And look to have it yielded with all willingness.
   Come, let us sup betimes, that afterwards   200
   We may digest our complots in some form.   *Exeunt*

SCENE II

Before Lord Hastings' house

Enter a Messenger

Messenger. What ho, my lord!
Hastings. (*within*) Who knocks [at the door?]
Messenger. A messenger from the Lord Stanley.

Enter Lord Hastings

Hastings. What is 't o'clock?
Messenger. Upon the stroke of four.
Hastings. Cannot thy master sleep these tedious nights?
Messenger. So it should seem by that I have to say.
   First, he commends him to your noble lordship.
Hastings. And then?
Messenger. And then he sends you word   10
   He dreamt to-night the boar had raz'd his helm:
   Besides, he says there are two councils held,
   And that may be determin'd at the one
   Which may make you and him to rue at the other;
   Therefore he sends to know your lordship's pleasure;
   If presently you will take horse with him,
   And with all speed post with him toward the north,
   To shun the danger that his soul divines.
Hastings. Go, fellow, go, return unto thy lord,
   Bid him not fear the separated councils: 20
   His honour and myself are at the one,
   And at the other is my servant Catesby;
   Where nothing can proceed that toucheth us,
   Whereof I shall not have intelligence.
   Tell him his fears are shallow, wanting instance,
   And for his dreams, I wonder he is so fond
   To trust the mockery of unquiet slumbers:

To fly the boar, before the boar pursues us,
Were to incense the boar to follow us,
And make pursuit where he did mean no chase.   30
Go, bid thy master rise and come to me,
And we will both together to the Tower,
Where he shall see the boar will use us kindly.
Messenger. My gracious lord, I'll tell him what you say.

Exit

Enter Catesby

Catesby. Many good morrows to my noble lord!
Hastings. Good morrow, Catesby, you are early stirring:
    What news, what news, in this our tottering state?
Catesby. It is a reeling world indeed, my lord;
    And I believe it will ne'er stand upright,
    Till Richard wear the garland of the realm.   40
Hastings. How? wear the garland? dost thou mean the
    crown?
Catesby. Ay, my good lord.
Hastings. I'll have this crown of mine cut from my
    shoulders,
    Ere I will see the crown so foul misplac'd.
    But canst thou guess that he doth aim at it?
Catesby. Upon my life, my lord, and hopes to find you for-
    ward
    Upon his party for the gain thereof;
    And thereupon he sends you this good news,
    That this same very day your enemies,
    The kindred of the queen, must die at Pomfret.   50
Hastings. Indeed, I am no mourner for that news,
    Because they have been still mine enemies:
    But, that I'll give my voice on Richard's side,
    To bar my master's heirs in true descent,   **6697**
    God knows I will not do it, to the death.
Catesby. God keep your lordship in that gracious mind!
Hastings. But I shall laugh at this a twelve-month hence,
    That they who brought me in my master's hate,
    I live to look upon their tragedy.
    I tell thee, Catesby,—   60

[*Catesby*. What, my lord?]

Hastings. Ere a fortnight make me elder,
  I'll send some packing, that yet think not on it.
Catesby. 'Tis a vile thing to die, my gracious lord,
  When men are unprepar'd and look not for it.
Hastings. O monstrous, monstrous! and so falls it out
  With Rivers, Vaughan, Grey, and so 'twill do
  With some men else, who think themselves as safe
  As thou, and I, who, as thou know'st are dear
  To princely Richard, and to Buckingham.   70
Catesby. The princes both make high account of you;
  (*aside*) For they account his head upon the bridge.   †
Hastings. I know they do, and I have well deserv'd it.

Enter the Earl of Derby

  What, my lord? where is your boar-spear, man?
  Fear you the boar, and go so unprovided?
Derby. My lord, good morrow; good morrow, Catesby:
  You may jest on; but, by the holy rood,
  I do not like these several councils, I.
Hastings. My lord,
  I hold my life as dear as [you do] yours,   80
  And never in my life, I do protest,
  Was it more precious to me than 'tis now:
  Think you, but that I know our state secure,
  I would be so triumphant as I am?
Derby. The lords at Pomfret, when they rode from London,
  Were jocund, and suppos'd their states was sure,
  And they indeed had no cause to mistrust;
  But yet you see how soon the day o'ercast.
  This sudden stab of rancour I misdoubt:
  Pray God, I say, I prove a needless coward!   90
  But come, my lord, shall we to the Tower?
Hastings. I go; but stay, hear you not the news?
  This day those men you talk'd of are beheaded.
Derby. They, for their truth, might better wear their heads,
  Than some that have accus'd them wear their hats.
  But come, my lord, let us away.

Enter [Hastings] a Pursuivant   †

Hastings. Go you before; I'll follow presently.
                    Exeunt Stanley and Catesby
Well met, Hastings! how goes the world with thee?
Pursuivant. The better that it please your lordship to ask.
Hastings. I tell thee, fellow, 'tis better with me now,   100
   Than when I met thee last where now we meet:
   Then was I going prisoner to the Tower,
   By the suggestion of the queen's allies;
   But now, I tell thee (keep it to thyself)
   This day those enemies are put to death,
   And I in better state than e'er I was.
Pursuivant. God hold it, to your honour's good content!
Hastings. Gramercy, Hastings; hold, spend thou that.
                    Gives him his purse
Pursuivant. God save your lordship.   *Exit*

Enter a Priest

{*Priest.* Well met, my lord; I am glad to see your honour.}   110
Hastings. What, Sir John, you are well met,   †
   I am beholding to you for your last day's exercise:
   Come the next Sabbath, and I will content you.
                    He whispers in his ear

Enter Buckingham

Buckingham. How now, Lord Chamberlain? What, talking
   with a priest?
   Your friends at Pomfret, they do need the priest;
   Your honour hath no shriving work in hand.
Hastings. Good faith, and when I met this holy man,
   Those men you talk of came into my mind.
   What, go you to the Tower, my lord?
Buckingham. I do, {my lord;} but long I shall not stay: 120
   I shall return before your lordship thence.
Hastings. 'Tis like enough, for I stay dinner there.
Buckingham. (*aside*) And supper too, although thou
   know'st it not.

53

Come, shall we go along?
{*Hastings.*   I'll wait upon your lordship.}
                                                      Exeunt

SCENE III

Pomfret Castle

*Enter Sir Richard Ratcliff, with halberds, carrying
Rivers, Grey, and Vaughan to death*

[*Ratcliff.* Come, bring forth the prisoners.]
Rivers. Sir Richard Ratcliff, let me tell thee this:
  To-day shalt thou behold a subject die
  For truth, for duty, and for loyalty.
Grey. God keep the prince from all the pack of you!
  A knot you are of damned blood-suckers.
{*Vaughan.* You live that shall cry woe for this hereafter.
Ratcliff. Dispatch; the limit of your lives is out.}
Rivers. O Pomfret, Pomfret! O thou bloody prison,
  Fatal and ominous to noble peers!   10
  Within the guilty closure of thy walls
  Richard the second here was hack'd to death;
  And, for more slander to thy dismal soul,
  We give thee up our guiltless bloods to drink.
Grey. Now Margaret's curse is fall'n upon our heads,
  For standing by, when Richard stabb'd her son.
Rivers. Then curs'd she Hastings, then curs'd she Bucking-
    ham,
  Then curs'd she Richard. O, remember, God,
  To hear her prayers for them, as now for us!
  And for my sister and her princely son,   20
  Be satisfied, dear God, with our true bloods,
  Which, as thou know'st, unjustly must be spilt.
Ratcliff. {Make haste; the hour of death is expiate.}   †
  [Come, come, dispatch, the limit of your lives is out.]
Rivers. Come, Grey, come, Vaughan, let us all embrace,
  And take our leave, until we meet in heaven.   *Exeunt*

The Tower of London

Enter Buckingham, Derby, Hastings, the Bishop of Ely,
Ratcliff, Lovel, with others, and take their seats at a table

Hastings. My lords, at once, the cause why we are met
   Is, to determine of the coronation.
   In God's name, say, when is the royal day?
Buckingham. Are all things fitting for that royal time?
Derby. It is, and wants but nomination.
Ely. To-morrow then I guess a happy time.
Buckingham. Who knows the lord protector's mind herein?
   Who is most inward with the noble duke?
Ely. Why, you, my lord, methinks you should soonest know
     his mind.
Buckingham. [Who, I, my lord?] We know each other's
   faces,   10
   But for our hearts, he knows no more of mine
   Than I of yours;
   Nor I no more of his, than you of mine.
   Lord Hastings, you and he are near in love.
Hastings. I thank his grace, I know he loves me well;
   But, for his purpose in the coronation,
   I have not sounded him, nor he deliver'd
   His grace's pleasure any way therein:
   But you, my noble lords, may name the time;
   And in the duke's behalf I'll give my voice.   20
   Which, I presume, he'll take in gentle part.

Enter Gloucester

Ely. Now in good time, here comes the duke himself.
Gloucester. My noble lords and cousins all, good morrow.
   I have been long a sleeper; but, I hope,
   My absence doth neglect no great designs,
   Which by my presence might have been concluded.
Buckingham. Had not you come upon your cue, my lord,
   William Lord Hastings had now pronounc'd your part,

I mean your voice for crowning of the king.

Gloucester. Than my Lord Hastings no man might be
    bolder;   30

    His lordship knows me well, and loves me well.

[*Hastings.* I thank your grace.]

Gloucester.   My Lord of Ely!

[*Ely.*   My lord?

Gloucester.] When I was last in Holborn,

    I saw good strawberries in your garden there:

    I do beseech you send for some of them.

Ely. [I go, my lord.]

    {Marry, and will, my lord, with all my heart.}   *Exit*

Gloucester. Cousin of Buckingham, a word with you.

                             Drawing him aside

    Catesby hath sounded Hastings in our business,

    And finds the testy gentleman so hot,   40

    As he will lose his head ere give consent

    His master's son, as worshipful he terms it,

    Shall lose the royalty of England's throne.

Buckingham. Withdraw you hence, my lord, I'll follow you.

             Exit Gloucester, Buckingham following

Derby. We have not yet set down this day of triumph.

    To-morrow, in mine opinion, is too sudden;

    For I myself am not so well provided

    As else I would be, were the day prolong'd.

                Re-enter Bishop of Ely

Ely. Where is my lord protector? I have sent for these
    strawberries.   50

Hastings. His grace looks cheerfully and smooth to-day;

    There's some conceit or other likes him well,

    When he doth bid good morrow with such a spirit.

    I think there's never a man in Christendom

    That can lesser hide his love or hate than he;

    For by his face straight shall you know his heart.

Derby. What of his heart perceive you in his face

    By any likelihood he show'd to-day?

Hastings. Marry, that with no man here he is offended;

For, if he were, he would have shown it in his looks.   60
[*Derby*. I pray God he be not, I say.]

Re-enter Gloucester and Buckingham

Gloucester. I pray you all, what do they deserve
  That do conspire my death with devilish plots
  Of damned witchcraft, and that have prevail'd
  Upon my body with their hellish charms?
Hastings. The tender love I bear your grace, my lord,
  Makes me most forward in this noble presence
  To doom the offenders, whatsoever they be:
  I say, my lord, they have deserved death.
Gloucester. Then be your eyes the witness of this ill: 70
  See how I am bewitch'd; behold, mine arm
  Is like a blasted sapling, withered up:
  And this is Edward's wife, that monstrous witch,
  Consorted with that harlot strumpet Shore,
  That by their witchcraft thus have marked me.
Hastings. If they have done this thing, my gracious lord,—
Gloucester. If? thou protector of this damned strumpet,
  Tellest thou me of 'ifs'? Thou art a traitor:
  Off with his head! Now, by Saint Paul   †
  I will not dine to-day, I swear,   80
  Until I see the same: some see it done,
  The rest that love me, come and follow me.

Exeunt all but Hastings, {Ratcliff and
Lovel} [and Catesby]

Hastings. Woe, woe for England, not a whit for me!
  For I, too fond, might have prevented this.
  Stanley did dream the boar did raze his helm,
  But I disdain'd it, and did scorn to fly:
  Three times to-day my foot-cloth horse did stumble,
  And startled, when he look'd upon the Tower,
  As loath to bear me to the slaughter-house.
  O, now I want the priest that spake to me,   90
  I now repent I told the pursuivant,
  As 'twere triumphing at mine enemies,
  How they at Pomfret bloodily were butcher'd,
  And I myself secure in grace and favour.

57

O Margaret, Margaret, now thy heavy curse
Is lighted on poor Hastings' wretched head!
Catesby. Dispatch, my lord; the duke would be at dinner:
Make a short shrift; he longs to see your head.
Hastings. O momentary state of worldly men,
Which we more hunt for than the grace of heaven!   100
Who builds his hopes in air of your fair looks,
Lives like a drunken sailor on a mast,
Ready, with every nod, to tumble down
Into the fatal bowels of the deep.
{*Lovel.* Come, come, dispatch; 'tis bootless to exclaim.
Hastings. O bloody Richard! miserable England!
I prophesy the fearfull'st time to thee
That ever wretched age hath look'd upon.}
Come, lead me to the block, bear him my head,
They smile at me that shortly shall be dead.   *Exeunt* 110

SCENE V

The Tower-walls

Enter Gloucester and Buckingham, in {rotten} armour,   †
{marvellous ill-favoured}

Gloucester. Come, cousin, canst thou quake, and change
       thy colour,
Murder thy breath in middle of a word,
And then begin again, and stop again,
As if thou wert distraught and mad with terror?
Buckingham. Tut, fear not me;
I can counterfeit the deep tragedian,
Speak and look back, and pry on every side,
{Tremble and start at wagging of a straw,}
Intending deep suspicion: ghastly looks
Are at my service, like enforced smiles;   10
And both are ready in their offices,
{At any time,} to grace my stratagems.
{But what, is Catesby gone?
Gloucester. He is; and, see, he brings the mayor along.}
[Here comes the mayor.]

Enter the Mayor {and Catesby}

Buckingham. [Let me alone to entertain him.] Lord
  mayor,—
Gloucester. Look to the drawbridge there!
Buckingham. The reason we have sent for you—
Gloucester. Catesby, o'erlook the walls.
Buckingham. Hark, I hear a drum.   20
Gloucester. Look back, defend thee, here are enemies.
Buckingham. God and our innocence defend us!
Gloucester. [O, o, be quiet, it is Catesby.]
    {Be patient, they are friends, Ratcliff and Lovel.}

          Enter {Lovel and Ratcliff} [Catesby] with
                      Hastings' head   †

Catesby. Here is the head of that ignoble traitor,
    The dangerous and unsuspected Hastings.
Gloucester. So dear I lov'd the man, that I must weep.
    I took him for the plainest harmless man
    That breathed upon this earth a Christian;
    [Look ye, my lord mayor—]   30
    Made him my book, wherein my soul recorded
    The history of all her secret thoughts:
    So smooth he daub'd his vice with show of virtue
    That, his apparent open guilt omitted,
    I mean, his conversation with Shore's wife,
    He laid from all attainder of suspect.
Buckingham. Well, well, he was the covert'st shelter'd traitor
    That ever lived: would you have imagined,
    Or almost believe, were 't not by great preservation,
    We live to tell it you; the subtle traitor   40
    This day had plotted, in the council-house
    To murder me and my good Lord of Gloucester?
Mayor. What, had he so?
Gloucester. What, think you we are Turks or infidels?
    Or that we would, against the form of law,
    Proceed thus rashly to the villain's death,
    But that the extreme peril of the case,
    The peace of England and our persons' safety,
    Enforc'd us to this execution?

                          59

Mayor. Now, fair befall you! he deserv'd his death,   50
   And you, my good lords both, have well proceeded,
   To warn false traitors from the like attempts.
   I never look'd for better at his hands,   †
   After he once fell in with Mistress Shore.
Gloucester. Yet had not we determin'd he should die,
   Until your lordship came to see his death,
   Which now the longing haste of these our friends,
   Somewhat against our meaning, have prevented:
   Because, my lord, we would have had you hear   †
   The traitor speak, and timorously confess   60
   The manner and the purpose of his treason,
   That you might well have signified the same
   Unto the citizens, who haply may
   Misconster us in him, and wail his death.
Mayor. But, my good lord, your grace's word shall serve,
   As well as I had seen and heard him speak,
   And doubt you not, right noble princes both,
   But I'll acquaint our duteous citizens
   With all your just proceedings in this cause.
Gloucester. And to that end we wish'd your lordship here,   70
   To avoid the carping censures of the world.
Buckingham. But since you come too late of our intents,
   Yet witness what we did intend, and so
   My lord, adieu.   *Exit Mayor*
Gloucester. After, after, cousin Buckingham.
   The mayor towards Guildhall hies him in all post:
   There, at your meet'st advantage of the time,
   Infer the bastardy of Edward's children:
   Tell them how Edward put to death a citizen,
   Only for saying he would make his son   80
   Heir to the Crown, meaning indeed his house,
   Which, by the sign thereof, was termed so.
   Moreover, urge his hateful luxury
   And bestial appetite in change of lust;
   Which stretched to their servants, daughters, wives,
   Even where his lustful eye, or savage heart,
   Without control listed to make his prey.
   Nay, for a need, thus far come near my person:

Tell them, when that my mother went with child
Of that unsatiate Edward, noble York,   90
My princely father, then had wars in France;
And, by just computation of the time,
Found that the issue was not his begot;
Which well appeared in his lineaments,
Being nothing like the noble duke my father:
But touch this sparingly, as 'twere far off;
Because you know, my lord, my mother lives.
Buckingham. Fear not, my lord, I'll play the orator,
   As if the golden fee for which I plead
   Were for myself: {and so, my lord, adieu.}   100
Gloucester. If you thrive well, bring them to Baynard's
      Castle,
   Where you shall find me well accompanied
   With reverend fathers and well-learned bishops.
Buckingham. [About three or four a clock look to hear
   What news Guildhall affordeth, and so, my lord, fare-
      well.]
   {I go; and towards three or four o'clock
   Look for the news that the Guildhall affords.}   *Exit*
Gloucester. {Go, Lovel, with all speed to Doctor Shaw;
   (*to Catesby*) Go thou to Friar Penker; bid them both
   Meet me within this hour at Baynard's Castle.}   110
                              Exeunt all but Gloucester
Now will I in, to take some privy order,
To draw the brats of Clarence out of sight;
And to give notice, that no manner of person
At any time have recourse unto the princes.   *Exit*

SCENE VI

The same. A street

Enter a Scrivener, with a paper in his hand

Scrivener. This is the indictment of the good Lord Has-
      tings;
   Which in a set hand fairly is engross'd,
   That it may be this day read o'er in Paul's.

And mark how well the sequel hangs together:
Eleven hours I spent to write it over,
For yesternight by Catesby was it brought me;
The precedent was full as long a-doing:
And yet within these five hours liv'd Lord Hastings,
Untainted, unexamin'd, free, at liberty.
Here's a good world the while! Why, who's so gross,　　10
That seeth not this palpable device?
Yet who's so blind, but says he sees it not?
Bad is the world, and all will come to nought,
When such bad dealing must be seen in thought.　　*Exit*

SCENE VII

Baynard's Castle

Enter Gloucester and Buckingham, at several doors

Gloucester. How now, my lord, what say the citizens?
Buckingham. Now, by the holy mother of our Lord,
　The citizens are mum, and speak not a word.
Gloucester. Touch'd you the bastardy of Edward's children?
Buckingham. I did; with {his contract with Lady Lucy,
　And his contract by deputy in France;}
　The insatiate greediness of his desires,
　{And his enforcement of the city wives;}
　His tyranny for trifles; his own bastardy,
　As being got, your father then in France,　　10
　{And his resemblance, being not like the duke:}
　Withal I did infer your lineaments,
　Being the right idea of your father,
　Both in your form and nobleness of mind;
　Laid open all your victories in Scotland,
　Your discipline in war, wisdom in peace,
　Your bounty, virtue, fair humility;
　Indeed left nothing fitting for the purpose
　Untouch'd or slightly handled in discourse:
　And when mine oratory grew to an end,　　20
　I bid them that did love their country's good
　Cry 'God save Richard, England's royal king!'
Gloucester. [Ah!] and did they so?

Buckingham. No, so God help me, {they spake not a word;}
  But, like dumb statuës or breathing stones,
  Gaz'd each on other, and look'd deadly pale.
  Which when I saw, I reprehended them;
  And ask'd the mayor what meant this wilful silence:
  His answer was, the people were not wont
  To be spoke to but by the recorder.   30
  Then he was urg'd to tell my tale again:
  'Thus saith the duke, thus hath the duke inferr'd;'
  But nothing spake in warrant from himself.
  When he had done, some followers of mine own
  At the lower end of the hall hurl'd up their caps.
  And some ten voices cried 'God save King Richard!'
  {And thus I took the vantage of those few,}
  'Thanks, loving citizens and friends!' quoth I,
  'This general applause and loving shout
  Argues your wisdoms and your love to Richard;'   40
  And so brake off, and came away.
Gloucester. What tongueless blocks were they! would they
     not speak?
[*Buckingham.* No, by my troth, my lord.]
Gloucester. Will not the mayor then and his brethren come?
Buckingham. The mayor is here at hand: intend some fear;
  Be not spoken withal, but with mighty suit:
  And look you get a prayer-book in your hand,
  And stand betwixt two churchmen, good my lord;
  For on that ground I'll build a holy descant:
  And be not easily won to our request;   50
  Play the maid's part, say no, but take it.
Gloucester. Fear not me; if thou canst plead as well for
     them
  As I can say nay to thee for myself,
  No doubt we'll bring it to a happy issue.
Buckingham. You shall see what I can do; get you up to the
     leads.   *Exit Gloucester*

             Enter the Mayor and Citizens

  Now, my lord mayor, I dance attendance here;
  I think the duke will not be spoke withal.

                         63

Enter Catesby

Here comes his servant: how now, Catesby,
What says he?
Catesby.　　　My lord, he doth entreat your grace
　　To visit him to-morrow or next day:　　　　　　　　60
　　He is within, with two right reverend fathers,
　　Divinely bent to meditation;
　　And in no wordly suit would he be mov'd,
　　To draw him from his holy exercise.
Buckingham. Return, good Catesby, to thy lord again,
　　Tell him, myself, the mayor and citizens,
　　In deep designs and matters of great moment,
　　No less importing that our general good,
　　Are come to have some conference with his grace.
Catesby. I'll tell him what you say, my lord.　　　*Exit*　70
Buckingham. Ah, ha, my lord, this prince is not an Edward!
　　He is not lolling on a lewd day-bed,
　　But on his knees at meditation;
　　Not dallying with a brace of courtezans,
　　But meditating with two deep divines;
　　Not sleeping, to engross his idle body,
　　But praying, to enrich his watchful soul:
　　Happy were England, would this gracious prince
　　Take on himself the sovereignty thereon:
　　But, sure, I fear, we shall ne'er win him to it.　　　80
Mayor. Marry, God forbid his grace should say us nay!
Buckingham. I fear he will. {Here Catesby comes again.}

Re-enter Catesby

How now, Catesby, what says your lord?
Catesby.　　　　　　　　　　[My lord,]
　　He wonders to what end you have assembled
　　Such troops of citizens to speak with him,
　　His grace not being warn'd thereof before:
　　My lord, he fears you mean no good to him.
Buckingham. Sorry I am my noble cousin should
　　Suspect me, that I mean no good to him:
　　By heaven, I come in perfect love to him:　　　　　90
　　And so once more return and tell his grace.　　*Exit Catesby*

64

When holy and devout religious men
Are at their beads, 'tis hard to draw them thence,
So sweet is zealous contemplation.

Enter Gloucester aloft, between two Bishops.

Catesby returns

Mayor. See, where he stands between two clergymen!
Buckingham. Two props of virtue for a Christian prince,
   To stay him from the fall of vanity:
   {And, see, a book of prayer in his hand,
   True ornaments to know a holy man.}
   Famous Plantagenet, most gracious prince,   100
   Lend favourable ears to our request;
   And pardon us the interruption
   Of thy devotion and right Christian zeal.
Gloucester. My lord, there needs no such apology:
   I rather do beseech you pardon me,
   Who, earnest in the service of my God,
   Neglect the visitation of my friends.
   But, leaving this, what is your grace's pleasure?
Buckingham. Even that, I hope, which pleaseth God above,
   And all good men of this ungovern'd isle.   110
Gloucester. I do suspect I have done some offence
   That seems disgracious in the city's eyes,
   And that you come to reprehend my ignorance.
Buckingham. You have, my lord: would it might please
     your grace,
   At our entreaties, to amend that fault!
Gloucester. Else wherefore breathe I in a Christian land?
Buckingham. Then know, it is your fault that you resign
   The supreme seat, the throne majestical,
   The scepter'd office of your ancestors,
   {Your state of fortune and your due of birth,}   120
   The lineal glory of your royal house,
   To the corruption of a blemish'd stock:
   Whilst, in the mildness of your sleepy thoughts,
   Which here we waken to our country's good,
   This noble isle doth want her proper limbs;
   Her face defac'd with scars of infamy,

{Her royal stock graft with ignoble plants,}
And almost shoulder'd in the swallowing gulf
Of blind forgetfulness and dark oblivion.
Which to recure, we heartily solicit   130
Your gracious self to take on you the sovereignty thereof,   †
Not as protector, steward, substitute,
Or lowly factor for another's gain;
But as successively, from blood to blood,
Your right of birth, your empery, your own.
For this, consorted with the citizens,
Your very worshipful and loving friends,
And by their vehement instigation,
In this just suit come I to move your grace.

Gloucester. I know not whether to depart in silence,   140
Or bitterly to speak in your reproof,
Best fitteth my degree or your condition:
{If not to answer, you might haply think
Tongue-tied ambition, not replying, yielded
To bear the golden yoke of sovereignty,
Which fondly you would here impose on me;
If to reprove you for this suit of yours
So season'd with your faithful love to me,
Then, on the other side, I check'd my friends.
Therefore, to speak, and to avoid the first,   150
And then in speaking, not to incur the last,
Definitively thus I answer you.}
Your love deserves my thanks, but my desert
Unmeritable shuns your high request.
First, if all obstacles were cut away,
And that my path were even to the crown,
As my ripe revenue and due by birth,
Yet so much is my poverty of spirit,
So mighty and so many my defects,
As I had rather hide me from my greatness,   160
Being a bark to brook no mighty sea,
Than in my greatness covet to be hid,
And in the vapour of my glory smother'd.
But, God be thanked, there's no need of me,
And much I need to help you, if need were;

The royal tree hath left us royal fruit,
Which, mellow'd by the stealing hours of time,
Will well become the seat of majesty,
And make, no doubt, us happy by his reign.
On him I lay what you would lay on me,   170
The right and fortune of his happy stars,
Which God defend that I should wring from him!
Buckingham. My lord, this argues conscience in your grace;
But the respects thereof are nice and trivial,
All circumstances well considered.
You say that Edward is your brother's son:
So say we too, but not by Edward's wife;
For first he was contract to Lady Lucy—
Your mother lives a witness to that vow—
And afterward by substitute betroth'd   180
To Bona, sister to the King of France.
These both put by, a poor petitioner,
A care-craz'd mother of a many children,
A beauty-waning and distressed widow,
Even in the afternoon of her best days,
Made prize and purchase of his lustful eye,   †
Seduc'd the pitch and height of all his thoughts
To base declension and loath'd bigamy:
By her, in his unlawful bed, he got
This Edward, whom our manners term the prince.   190
More bitterly could I expostulate,
Save that, for reverence to some alive,
I give a sparing limit to my tongue.
Then, good my lord, take to your royal self
This proffer'd benefit of dignity;
If not to bless us and the land withal,
Yet to draw out your royal stock
From the corruption of abusing time,
Unto a lineal true-derived course.
Mayor. Do, good my lord, your citizens entreat you.   200
{*Buckingham.* Refuse not, mighty lord, this proffer'd love.}
Catesby. O, make them joyful, grant their lawful suit!
Gloucester. Alas, why would you heap these cares on me:
    I am unfit for state and dignity:

I do beseech you, take it not amiss,
I cannot nor I will not yield to you.
Buckingham. If you refuse it, as, in love and zeal,
  Loath to depose the child, your brother's son,
  As well we know your tenderness of heart,
  And gentle, kind, effeminate remorse,   210
  Which we have noted in you to your kin,
  And equally indeed to all estates,—
  Yet whether you accept our suit or no,
  Your brother's son shall never reign our king,
  But we will plant some other in the throne,
  To the disgrace and downfall of your house:
  And in this resolution here we leave you.
  Come, citizens: 'zounds! I'll entreat no more.
[*Gloucester.* O, do not swear, my lord of Buckingham.]   †
           Exit Buckingham with the Citizens
Catesby. Call them again, my lord, and accept their suit: 220
Another. Do, good my lord, lest all the land do rue it.
Gloucester. Would you enforce me to a world of care?
  [Well,] call them again; I am not made of stones,
  But penetrable to your kind entreats,
  Albeit against my conscience and my soul.

        Re-enter Buckingham and the rest

  Cousin of Buckingham, and you sage, grave men,
  Since you will buckle fortune on my back,
  To bear her burthen, whether I will or no,
  I must have patience to endure the load;
  But if black scandal or foul-fac'd reproach   230
  Attend the sequel of your imposition,
  Your mere enforcement shall acquittance me
  From all the impure blots and stains thereof;
  For God he knows, and you may partly see,
  How far I am from the desire thereof.
Mayor. God bless your grace! we see it, and will say it.
Gloucester. In saying so, you shall but say the truth.
Buckingham. Then I salute you with this kingly title:
  Long live Richard, England's royal king!
Mayor and Citizens. Amen.   240

Buckingham. To-morrow will it please you to be crown'd?
Gloucester. Even when you will, since you will have it so.
Buckingham. To-morrow then we will attend your grace:
   {And so most joyfully we take our leave.}
Gloucester. Come, let us to our holy task again.
   Farewell, good cousin; farewell, gentle friends.   *Exeunt*

Act Fourth

SCENE I

Before the Tower

Enter, on one side, Queen Elizabeth, Duchess of York, and
Marquess of Dorset; on the other, Anne, Duchess of Gloucester,
{leading Lady Margaret Plantagenet, Clarence's young daughter} †

Duchess. Who meets us here? my niece Plantagenet
   {Led in the hand of her kind aunt of Gloucester?
   Now, for my life, she's wandering to the Tower,
   On pure heart's love to greet the tender prince.
   Daughter, well met.
Lady Anne.   God give your graces both
   A happy and a joyful time of day!
Queen Eliz. As much to you, good sister! Whither away?}
[*Queen.* Sister, well met; whither away so fast?]
Lady Anne. No farther than the Tower, and, as I guess,
   Upon the like devotion as yourselves,   10
   To gratulate the tender princes there.
Queen Eliz. Kind sister, thanks: we'll enter all together.

Enter Brakenbury

   And, in good time, here the lieutenant comes.
   Master lieutenant, pray you, by your leave,
   How fares the prince, {and my young son of York?}
Brakenbury. {Right well, dear madam. By your patience,}
   [Well, madam, and in health; but, by your leave,]

I may not suffer you to visit them;
The king hath straitly charged the contrary.
Queen Eliz. The king? why, who's that?   20
Brakenbury. [I cry you mercy:] I mean the lord protector.
Queen Eliz. The Lord protect him from that kingly title!
Hath he set bounds betwixt their love and me?
I am their mother, who should keep me from them?
Duchess. I am their father's mother, I will see them.
Lady Anne. Their aunt I am in law, in love their mother:
Then fear not thou; I'll bear thy blame,
And take thy office from thee, on my peril.
Brakenbury. I do beseech your graces all to pardon me;   †
I am bound by oath, I may not do it.   *Exit* 30

Enter the Earl of Derby

Derby. Let me but meet you, ladies, an hour hence,
And I'll salute your grace of York as mother,
And reverend looker on, of two fair queens.
(*to Anne*) Come, madam, you must straight to West-
minster,
There to be crowned, Richard's royal queen.
Queen Eliz. O, cut my lace in sunder, that my pent heart
May have some scope to beat, or else I swoon
With this dead-killing news!
{*Lady Anne.* Despiteful tidings! O unpleasing news!}
Dorset. Madam, have comfort, how fares your grace?   40
Queen Eliz. O Dorset, speak not to me, get thee hence!
Death and destruction dog thee at the heels;
Thy mother's name is ominous to children,
If thou wilt outstrip death, go cross the seas,
And live with Richmond, from the reach of hell:
Go, hie thee, hie thee from this slaughter-house,
Lest thou increase the number of the dead;
And make me die the thrall of Margaret's curse,
Nor mother, wife, nor England's counted queen.
Derby. Full of wise care is this your counsel, madam.   50
Take all the swift advantage of the time;
You shall have letters from me to my son
To meet you on the way, and welcome you.   †

Be not ta'en tardy by unwise delay.

Duchess. O ill-dispersing wind of misery!
 O my accursed womb, the bed of death,
 A cockatrice hast thou hatch'd to the world,
 Whose unavoided eye is murderous.

Derby. Come, madam, {come,} I in all haste was sent.

Lady Anne. And I in all unwillingness will go.   60
 I would to God that the inclusive verge
 Of golden metal that must round my brow
 Were red-hot steel, to sear me to the brain!
 Anointed let me be with deadly poison,
 And die, ere men can say, God save the queen!

Queen Eliz. Alas, poor soul, I envy not thy glory;
 To feed my humour, wish thyself no harm.

Lady Anne. No! {why?} When he that is my husband now
 Came to me, as I follow'd Henry's corse,
 When scarce the blood was well wash'd from his hands 70
 Which issued from my other angel husband,
 And that dead saint, which then I weeping follow'd;
 O, when, I say, I look'd on Richard's face,
 This was my wish: 'Be thou,' quoth I, 'accurs'd,
 For making me, so young, so old a widow!
 And, when thou wed'st, let sorrow haunt thy bed,
 And be thy wife, if any be so mad,
 As miserable by the death of thee
 As thou hast made me by my dear lord's death!'
 Lo, ere I can repeat this curse again,   80
 Even in so short a space, my woman's heart
 Grossly grew captive to his honey words,
 And prov'd the subject of my own soul's curse,
 Which ever since hath kept my eyes from sleep;
 For never yet one hour in his bed
 Have I enjoy'd the golden dew of sleep.
 But have been waked by his timorous dreams.
 Besides, he hates me for my father Warwick;
 And will, no doubt, shortly be rid of me.

Queen Eliz. Alas, poor soul, I pity thy complaints. 90

Lady Anne. No more than from my soul I mourn for yours.

Dorset. Farewell, thou woful welcomer of glory!

71

Lady Anne. Adieu, poor soul, that tak'st thy leave of it!

Duchess. (*to Dorset*) Go thou to Richmond, and good fortune guide thee!

(*to Anne*) Go thou to Richard, and good angels guard thee!

(*to Queen Elizabeth*) Go thou to sanctuary, good thoughts possess thee!

I to my grave, where peace and rest lie with me!

Eighty odd years of sorrow have I seen,

And each hour's joy wreck'd with a week of teen.

{*Queen Eliz.* Stay, yet look back with me unto the Tower.   100

Pity, you ancient stones, those tender babes,

Whom envy hath immur'd within your walls,

Rough cradle for such little pretty ones,

Rude ragged nurse, old sullen playfellow,

For tender princes: use my babies well!

So foolish sorrow bids your stones farewell.}   *Exeunt*

SCENES II AND III

London. The palace

Sennet. Enter Richard, in pomp, crowned; Buckingham, Catesby, a Page, and others

King Richard. Stand all apart. Cousin of Buckingham!

{*Buckingham.* My gracious sovereign?}

King Richard. Give me thy hand. (*Here he ascendeth the throne.*)

Thus high, by thy advice

And thy assistance, is king Richard seated:

But shall we wear these honours for a day?

Or shall they last, and we rejoice in them?

Buckingham. Still live they, and for ever may they last!

King Richard. O Buckingham, now do I play the touch,   †

To try if thou be current gold indeed:

Young Edward lives: think now what I would say.   10

Buckingham. Say on, my gracious sovereign.

King Richard. Why, Buckingham, I say, I would be king.

72

Buckingham. Why, so you are, my thrice renowned liege.
King Richard. Ha! am I king? 'tis so: but Edward lives.
Buckingham. True, noble prince.
King Richard.   O bitter consequence,
  That Edward still should live true noble prince!
  Cousin, thou wert not wont to be so dull:
  Shall I be plain? I wish the bastards dead;
  And I would have it suddenly perform'd.
  What sayest thou? speak suddenly; be brief.   20
Buckingham. Your grace may do your pleasure.
King Richard. Tut, tut, thou art all ice, thy kindness freezeth,
  Say, have I thy consent that they shall die?
Buckingham. Give me some breath, some little pause, my lord,
  Before I positively speak herein:
  I will resolve your grace immediately.   *Exit*
Catesby. (*aside*) The king is angry: see, he bites the lip.
King Richard. I will converse with iron-witted fools
  And unrespective boys: none are for me
  That look into me with considerate eyes: 30
  High-reaching Buckingham grows circumspect.
  Boy!
Page. My lord?
King Richard. Know'st thou not any whom corrupting gold
  Would tempt unto a close exploit of death?
Page. [My lord,] I know a discontented gentleman,
  Whose humble means match not his haughty mind:
  Gold were as good as twenty orators,
  And will, no doubt, tempt him to any thing.
King Richard. What is his name?
Page.   His name, my lord, is Tyrrel.   40
King Richard. {I partly know the man:} go, call him hither
  [presently].   *Exit Page*
  The deep-revolving witty Buckingham
  No more shall be the neighbour to my counsel:
  Hath he so long held out with me untir'd,
  And stops he now for breath? {Well, be it so!}

Enter Derby

How now! what news with you?   †
Derby. My lord, I hear the Marquis Dorset's fled
　To Richmond, in those parts beyond the seas
　Where he abides.   *Stands apart*
King Richard. {Come hither} Catesby.   50
[*Catesby.* My lord?]
King Richard. Rumour it abroad
　That Anne, my wife, is sick and like to die:
　I will take order for her keeping close.
　Inquire me out some mean-born gentleman,
　Whom I will marry straight to Clarence' daughter:
　The boy is foolish, and I fear not him.
　Look, how thou dream'st! I say again, give out
　That Anne my wife is sick, and like to die:
　About it, for it stands me much upon,   60
　To stop all hopes whose growth may damage me.
                                    Exit Catesby

　I must be married to my brother's daughter,
　Or else my kingdom stands on brittle glass.
　Murder her brothers, and then marry her!
　Uncertain way of gain, but I am in
　So far in blood that sin will pluck on sin:
　Tear-falling pity dwells not in this eye.

Re-enter Page, with Tyrrel

Is thy name Tyrrel?
Tyrrel. James Tyrrel, and your most obedient subject.
King Richard. Art thou, indeed?
Tyrrel.   Prove me, my gracious sovereign.   70
King Richard. Dar'st thou resolve to kill a friend of mine?
Tyrrel. Ay, my lord;
　But I had rather kill two enemies.
King Richard. Why, there thou hast it: two deep enemies,
　Foes to my rest, and my sweet sleep's disturbs,
　Are they that I would have thee deal upon:
　Tyrrel, I mean those bastards in the Tower.
Tyrrel. Let me have open means to come to them,

And soon I'll rid you from the fear of them.

King Richard. Thou sing'st sweet music. {Hark,} come
    hither, Tyrrel: 80
  Go, by that token: rise, and lend thine ear: *Whispers*
  'Tis no more but so: say it is done,
  And I will love thee, and prefer thee too.

[*Tyrrel.* 'Tis done, my gracious lord.

King Richard. Shall we hear from thee, Tyrrel, ere we
    sleep?

Tyrrel. Ye shall, my lord.] {I will dispatch it straight.}

                                             Exit

Re-enter Buckingham

Buckingham. My lord, I have consider'd in my mind
  The late demand that you did sound me in.

King Richard. Well, let that pass; Dorset is fled to Rich-
    mond.

Buckingham. I hear that news, my lord.   90

King Richard. Stanley, he is your wife's son: well, look to it.

Buckingham. My lord, I claim your gift, my due by promise,
  For which your honour and your faith is pawn'd,
  The earldom of Hereford and the moveables
  The which you promised I should possess.

King Richard. Stanley, look to your wife; if she convey
  Letters to Richmond, you shall answer it.

Buckingham. What says your highness to my just demand?

King Richard. As I remember, Henry the Sixth
  Did prophesy that Richmond should be king,   100
  When Richmond was a little peevish boy.
  A king, perhaps, [perhaps,]—

[*Buckingham.* My lord!

King Richard. How chance the prophet could not at that
    time
  Have told me, I being by, that I should kill him?

Buckingham. My lord, your promise for the earldom,—

King Richard. Richmond! When last I was at Exeter,
  The mayor in courtesy show'd me the castle,
  And call'd it Rougemont: at which name I started,
  Because a bard of Ireland told me once,   110

I should not live long after I saw Richmond.
Buckingham. My lord!
King Richard. Ay, what's o'clock?
Buckingham. I am thus bold to put your grace in mind
  Of what you promis'd me.
King Richard.   Well, but what's o'clock?
Buckingham. Upon the stroke of ten.
King Richard.   Well, let it strike.
Buckingham. Why let it strike?
King Richard. Because that, like a Jack, thou keep'st the
  stroke
  Betwixt thy begging and my meditation.
  I am not in the giving vein to day.   120
Buckingham. Why, then resolve me whether you will or
  no.]
{*Buckingham.* May it please you to resolve me in my suit.}
King Richard. [Tut, tut,]
  Thou troublest me; I am not in the vein.
                        Exeunt all but Buckingham
Buckingham. Is it even so? rewards he my true service
  With such deep contempt? made I him king for this?
  O, let me think on Hastings, and be gone
  To Brecknock, while my fearful head is on!   *Exit*

Enter Tyrrel

Tyrrel. The tyrannous and bloody deed is done,
  The most arch act of piteous massacre
  That ever yet this land was guilty of.
  Dighton and Forrest, whom I did suborn
  To do this ruthless piece of butchery,
  Although they were flesh'd villains, bloody dogs,
  Melting with tenderness and kind compassion,
  Wept like two children in their deaths' sad stories.
  'Lo, thus,' quoth Dighton, 'lay those tender babes:'
  'Thus, thus,' quoth Forrest, 'girdling one another   10

Within their innocent alabaster arms:
Their lips were four red roses on a stalk,
Which in their summer beauty kiss'd each other;
A book of prayers on their pillow lay,
Which once,' quoth Forrest, 'almost chang'd my mind;
But O! the devil'—there the villain stopp'd;
Whilst Dighton thus told on: 'We smothered
The most replenished sweet work of nature
That from the prime creation e'er she fram'd.'
Thus both are gone with conscience and remorse;   20
They could not speak; and so I left them both,
To bring this tidings to the bloody king.
And here he comes.

Enter King Richard

                    All hail, my sovereign liege!
King Richard. Kind Tyrrel, am I happy in thy news?
Tyrrel. If to have done the thing you give in charge
  Beget your happiness, be happy then,
  For it is done, [my lord.]
King Richard.   But didst thou see them dead?
Tyrrel. I did, my lord.
King Richard.   And buried, gentle Tyrrel?
Tyrrel. The chaplain of the Tower hath buried them;
  But how or in what place I do not know.   †
King Richard. Come to me, Tyrrel, soon at after supper, 31
  And thou shalt tell the process of their death.
  Meantime, but think how I may do thee good,
  And be inheritor of thy desire.
  Farewell till soon.
{*Tyrrel.*   I humbly take my leave.}   *Exit Tyrrel*
King Richard. The son of Clarence have I pent up close;
  His daughter meanly have I match'd in marriage;
  The sons of Edward sleep in Abraham's bosom,
  And Anne my wife hath bid the world good night.
  Now, for I know the Breton Richmond aims   40
  At young Elizabeth, my brother's daughter,
  And, by that knot, looks proudly o'er the crown,
  To her I go, a jolly thriving wooer.

Enter [Catesby] {Ratcliff}

Catesby. My lord!

King Richard. Good news or bad, that thou comest in so
    bluntly?

Catesby. Bad news, my lord: Ely is fled to Richmond;
    And Buckingham, back'd with the hardy Welshmen,
    Is in the field, and still his power increaseth.

King Richard. Ely with Richmond troubles me more near
    Than Buckingham and his rash-levied army.   50
    Come, I have heard that fearful commenting
    Is leaden servitor to dull delay;
    Delay leads impotent and snail-pac'd beggary:
    Then fiery expedition be my wing,
    Jove's Mercury, and herald for a king!
    Come, muster men, my counsel is my shield,
    We must be brief when traitors brave the field.

Exeunt

SCENE IV

Before the palace

Enter Queen Margaret

Queen Mar. So, now prosperity begins to mellow
    And drop into the rotten mouth of death.
    Here in these confines slily have I lurk'd,
    To watch the waning of mine adversaries.   †
    A dire induction am I witness to,
    And will to France, hoping the consequence
    Will prove as bitter, black, and tragical.
    Withdraw thee, wretched Margaret: who comes here?

Enter Queen Elizabeth and the Duchess of York

Queen Eliz. Ah, my young princes! ah, my tender babes!
    My unblown flowers, new-appearing sweets!   10
    If yet your gentle souls fly in the air,
    And be not fix'd in doom perpetual,
    Hover about me with your airy wings,
    And hear your mother's lamentation!

Queen Mar. Hover about her; say, that right for right
   Hath dimm'd your infant morn to aged night.
{*Duchess.* So many miseries have craz'd my voice,
   That my woe-wearied tongue is still and mute.
   Edward Plantagenet, why art thou dead?
Queen Mar. Plantagenet doth quit Plantagenet,   20
   Edward for Edward pays a dying debt.}
Queen Eliz. Wilt thou, O God, fly from such gentle lambs,
   And throw them in the entrails of the wolf?
   When didst thou sleep when such a deed was done?
Queen Mar. When holy Harry died, and my sweet son.
Duchess. Blind sight, dead life, poor mortal living ghost,
   Woe's scene, world's shame, grave's due by life usurp'd,
   {Brief abstract and record of tedious days,}
   Rest thy unrest on England's lawful earth,   *Sitting down*
   Unlawfully made drunk with innocents' blood!   30
Queen Eliz. O, that thou wouldst as well afford a grave
   As thou canst yield a melancholy sea!
   Then would I hide my bones, not rest them here.
   O, who hath any cause to mourn but I?
                    Sitting down by her
[*Duchess.* So many miseries have craz'd my voice,
   That my woe-wearied tongue is mute and dumb.
   Edward Plantagenet, why art thou dead?]
Queen Mar. If ancient sorrow be most reverend,
   Give mine the benefit of signory,
   And let my woes frown on the upper hand.   40
   If sorrow can admit society,   *Sitting down with them*
   [Tell o'er your woes again by viewing mine:]
   I had an Edward, till a Richard kill'd him;
   I had a Harry, till a Richard kill'd him:
   Thou hadst an Edward, till a Richard kill'd him;
   Thou hadst a Richard, till a Richard kill'd him.
Duchess. I had a Richard too, and thou didst kill him;
   I had a Rutland too, thou holp'st to kill him.
Queen Mar. Thou hadst a Clarence too, and Richard kill'd
    him.
   From forth the kennel of thy womb hath crept   50
   A hell-hound that doth hunt us all to death:

That dog, that had his teeth before his eyes,
To worry lambs, and lap their gentle bloods,
That foul defacer of God's handiwork,
{That reigns in galled eyes of weeping souls,
That excellent grand tyrant of the earth,}
Thy womb let loose, to chase us to our graves.
O upright, just, and true-disposing God,
How do I thank thee, that this carnal cur
Preys on the issue of his mother's body,   60
And makes her pew-fellow with others' moan!

Duchess. O Harry's wife, triumph not in my woes!
God witness with me, I have wept for thine.

Queen Mar. Bear with me; I am hungry for revenge,
And now I cloy me with beholding it.
Thy Edward he is dead, that stabb'd my Edward,
Thy other Edward dead, to quit my Edward,
Young York he is but boot, because both they
Match not the high perfection of my loss;
Thy Clarence he is dead that kill'd my Edward,   70
And the beholders of this tragic play,
The adulterate Hastings, Rivers, Vaughan, Grey,
Untimely smother'd in their dusky graves.
Richard yet lives, hell's black intelligencer,
Only reserv'd their factor, to buy souls
And send them thither: but at hand, at hand,
Ensues his piteous and unpitied end:
Earth gapes, hell burns, fiends roar, saints pray,
To have him suddenly convey'd away.
Cancel his bond of life, dear God, I pray,   80
That I may live to say, The dog is dead!

Queen Eliz. O, thou didst prophesy the time would come
That I should wish for thee to help me curse
That bottled spider, that foul bunch-back'd toad!

Queen Mar. I call'd thee then vain flourish of my fortune;
I call'd thee then poor shadow, painted queen,
The presentation of but what I was,
The flattering index of a direful pageant;
One heav'd a-high, to be hurl'd down below,
A mother only mock'd with two sweet babes,   90

A dream of what thou wert, a breath, a bubble,
A sign of dignity, a garish flag,
To be the aim of every dangerous shot,
A queen in jest, only to fill the scene.
Where is thy husband now? where be thy brothers?
Where are thy children? wherein dost thou joy?
Who sues to thee, and cries 'God save the queen'?
Where be the bending peers that flatter'd thee?
Where be the thronging troops that follow'd thee?
Decline all this, and see what now thou art;   100
For happy wife, a most distressed widow,
For joyful mother, one that wails the name,
For queen, a very caitiff crown'd with care,
For one being sued to, one that humbly sues,
For one commanding all, obey'd of none.
{For one being fear'd of all, now fearing one;}
For one that scorn'd at me, now scorn'd of me,
Thus hath the course of justice wheel'd about,
And left thee but a very prey to time,
Having no more but thought of what thou wert,   110
To torture thee the more, being what thou art;
Thou didst usurp my place, and dost thou not
Usurp the just proportion of my sorrow?
Now thy proud neck bears half my burthen'd yoke,
From which, even here, I slip my weary neck,   †
And leave the burthen of it all on thee.
Farewell, York's wife, and queen of sad mischance:
These English woes will make me smile in France.
Queen Eliz. O thou well skill'd in curses, stay awhile,
And teach me how to curse mine enemies!   120
Queen Mar. Forbear to sleep the nights, and fast the days,
Compare dead happiness with living woe,
Think that thy babes were fairer than they were,
And he that slew them fouler than he is;
Bettering thy loss makes the bad causer worse:
Revolving this will teach thee how to curse.
Queen Eliz. My words are dull, O, quicken them with
    thine!

81

Queen Mar. Thy woes will make them sharp, and pierce
    like mine.   *Exit*

Duchess. Why should calamity be full of words?

Queen Eliz. Windy attorneys to your client woes,   130
    Airy succeeders of intestate joys,
    Poor breathing orators of miseries,
    Let them have scope: though what they do impart
    Help not at all, yet do they ease the heart.

Duchess. If so, then be not tongue-tied: go with me,
    And in the breath of bitter words let's smother
    My damned son, which thy two sweet sons smother'd.
    I hear his drum: be copious in exclaims.   †

    Enter King Richard, marching, with drums and trumpets

King Richard. Who intercepts my expedition?

Duchess. Ah, she that might have intercepted thee,   140
    By strangling thee in her accursed womb,
    From all the slaughters, wretch, that thou hast done!

Queen Eliz. Hid'st thou that forehead with a golden crown,
    Where should be graven, if that right were right,
    The slaughter of the prince that owed that crown,
    And the dire death of my two sons and brothers?
    Tell me, thou villain slave, where are my children?

Duchess. Thou toad, thou toad, where is thy brother
    Clarence?
    And little Ned Plantagenet, his son?

Queen Eliz. Where is kind Hastings, Rivers, Vaughan,
    Grey?   150

King Richard. A flourish, trumpets! strike alarum, drums!
    Let not the heavens hear these tell-tale women
    Rail on the Lord's anointed: strike, I say!

                           Flourish. Alarums
    Either be patient, and entreat me fair,
    Or with the clamorous report of war
    Thus will I drown your exclamations.

Duchess. Art thou my son?

King Richard. Ay, I thank God, my father, and yourself.

Duchess. Then patiently hear my impatience.

King Richard. Madam, I have a touch of your condition,   160

Which cannot brook the accent of reproof.
{*Duchess.* O, let me speak!
King Richard.   Do then; but I'll not hear.}
Duchess. I will be mild and gentle in my speech.
King Richard. And brief, good mother, for I am in haste.
Duchess. Art thou so hasty? I have stay'd for thee,
　God knows, in anguish, pain and agony.
King Richard. And came I not at last to comfort you?
Duchess. No, by the holy rood, thou know'st it well,
　Thou cam'st on earth to make the earth my hell.
　A grievous burthen was thy birth to me,　　　　　170
　Tetchy and wayward was thy infancy,
　Thy school-days frightful, desperate, wild, and furious,
　Thy prime of manhood daring, bold, and venturous,
　Thy age confirm'd, proud, subtle, bloody, treacherous;
　{More mild, but yet more harmful, kind in hatred:}
　What comfortable hour canst thou name,
　That ever grac'd me in thy company?
King Richard. Faith, none, but Humphrey Hour, that call'd　　†
　　your grace
　To breakfast once forth of my company.
　If I be so disgracious in your sight,　　　　　180
　Let me march on, and not offend your grace.
　{Strike up the drum.
Duchess.　　　　　I prithee, hear me speak.
King Richard. You speak too bitterly.
Duchess.　　　　　　　　Hear me a word;
　For I shall never speak to thee again.
King Richard. So.}
[*Duchess.* O hear me speak, for I shall never see thee more.
King Richard. Come, come, you are too bitter.]
Duchess. Either thou wilt die, by God's just ordinance,
　Ere from this war thou turn a conqueror,
　Or I with grief and extreme age shall perish,　　　190
　And never look upon thy face again.
　Therefore take with thee my most heavy curse,
　Which, in the day of battle, tire thee more
　Than all the complete armour that thou wear'st!
　My prayers on the adverse party fight,

And there the little souls of Edward's children
Whisper the spirits of thine enemies,
And promise them success and victory.
Bloody thou art, bloody will be thy end;
Shame serves thy life and doth thy death attend.   200

Exit

Queen Eliz. Though far more cause, yet much less spirit to
    curse
Abides in me; I say amen to all.
King Richard. Stay, madam; I must speak a word with you.
Queen Eliz. I have no moe sons of the royal blood
    For thee to murder: for my daughters, Richard,
    They shall be praying nuns, not weeping queens;
    And therefore level not to hit their lives.
King Richard. You have a daughter call'd Elizabeth,
    Virtuous and fair, royal and gracious.
Queen Eliz. And must she die for this? O, let her live,   210
    And I'll corrupt her manners, stain her beauty,
    Slander myself as false to Edward's bed,
    Throw over her the veil of infamy;
    So she may live unscarr'd from bleeding slaughter,
    I will confess she was not Edward's daughter.
King Richard. Wrong not her birth, she is of royal blood.
Queen Eliz. To save her life, I'll say she is not so.
King Richard. Her life is only safest in her birth.
Queen Eliz. And only in that safety died her brothers.
King Richard. Lo, at their births good stars were oppo-
    site.   220
Queen Eliz. No, to their lives bad friends were contrary.
King Richard. All unavoided is the doom of destiny.
Queen Eliz. True, when avoided grace makes destiny:
    My babes were destin'd to a fairer death,
    If grace had bless'd thee with a fairer life.
{*King Richard.* You speak as if that I had slain my cousins.
Queen Eliz. Cousins, indeed; and by their uncle cozen'd
    Of comfort, kingdom, kindred, freedom, life.
    Whose hand soever lanc'd their tender hearts,
    Thy head, all indirectly, gave direction: 230
    No doubt the murderous knife was dull and blunt,

Till it was whetted on thy stone-hard heart,
To revel in the entrails of my lambs.
But that still use of grief makes wild grief tame,
My tongue should to thy ears not name my boys,
Till that my nails were anchor'd in thine eyes;
And I, in such a desperate bay of death,
Like a poor bark, of sails and tackling reft,
Rush all to pieces on thy rocky bosom.}

King Richard. Madam,   240
  So thrive I in my dangerous attempt   †
  Of hostile arms,
  As I intend more good to you and yours,
  Than ever you or yours were by me wrong'd!

Queen Eliz. What good is cover'd with the face of heaven,
  To be discover'd, that can do me good?

King Richard. The advancement of your children, mighty
    lady.

Queen Eliz. Up to some scaffold, there to lose their heads.

King Richard. No, to the dignity and height of honour,
  The high imperial type of this earth's glory.   250

Queen Eliz. Flatter my sorrows with report of it;
  Tell me what state, what dignity, what honour,
  Canst thou demise to any child of mine?

King Richard. Even all I have, yea, and myself and all,
  Will I withal endow a child of thine;
  So in the Lethe of thy angry soul
  Thou drown the sad remembrance of those wrongs
  Which thou supposest I have done to thee.

Queen Eliz. Be brief, lest that the process of thy kindness
  Last longer telling than thy kindness do.   260

King Richard. Then know, that from my soul I love thy
    daughter.

Queen Eliz. My daughter's mother thinks it with her soul.

King Richard. What do you think?

Queen Eliz. That thou dost love my daughter from thy soul,   †
  So from thy soul's love didst thou love her brothers,
  And from my heart's love I do thank thee for it.

King Richard. Be not so hasty to confound my meaning:
  I mean, that with my soul I love thy daughter,

And mean to make her queen of England.

Queen Eliz. Say then, who dost thou mean shall be her
    king? 270

King Richard. Even he that makes her queen; who should
    be else?

Queen Eliz. What, thou?

King Richard. Ay, even I: what think you of it, madam?

Queen Eliz. How canst thou woo her?

King Richard.   That would I learn of you,
    As one that are best acquainted with her humour.

Queen Eliz. And wilt thou learn of me?

King Richard.   Madam, with all my heart.

Queen Eliz. Send to her, by the man that slew her brothers,
    A pair of bleeding hearts; thereon engrave
    Edward and York; then haply she will weep:
    Therefore present to her,—as sometime Margaret 280
    Did to thy father, [a handkerchief] steep'd in Rutland's
    blood,—
    {A handkerchief; which, say to her, did drain
    The purple sap from her sweet brother's body,}
    And bid her dry her weeping eyes therewith.
    If this inducement force her not to love,
    Send her a story of thy noble acts;
    Tell her thou mad'st away her uncle Clarence,
    Her uncle Rivers; yea, and, for her sake,
    Mad'st quick conveyance with her good aunt Anne.

King Richard. Come, come, you mock me, this is not the
    way 290
    To win your daughter.

Queen Eliz.   There is no other way;
    Unless thou couldst put on some other shape,
    And not be Richard that hath done all this.

{*King Richard.* Say that I did all this for love of her.

Queen Eliz. Nay, then indeed she cannot choose but hate
    thee,
    Having bought love with such a bloody spoil.

King Richard. Look, what is done cannot be now amended:
    Men shall deal unadvisedly sometimes,
    Which after-hours gives leisure to repent.

If I did take the kingdom from your sons,   300
To make amends, I'll give it to your daughter.
If I have kill'd the issue of your womb,
To quicken your increase, I will beget
Mine issue of your blood upon your daughter:
A grandam's name is little less in love
Than is the doting title of a mother;
They are as children but one step below,
Even of your mettle, of your very blood;
Of all one pain, save for a night of groans
Endur'd of her, for whom you bid like sorrow.   310
Your children were vexation to your youth,
But mine shall be a comfort to your age.
The loss you have is but a son being king,
And by that loss your daughter is made queen.
I cannot make you what amends I would,
Therefore accept such kindness as I can.
Dorset your son, that with a fearful soul
Leads discontented steps in foreign soil,
This fair alliance quickly shall call home
To high promotions, and great dignity: 320
The king, that calls your beauteous daughter wife,
Familiarly shall call thy Dorset brother;
Again shall you be mother to a king;
And all the ruins of distressful times
Repair'd with double riches of content.
What? we have many goodly days to see:
The liquid drops of tears that you have shed
Shall come again, transform'd to orient pearl,
Advantaging their loan with interest
Of ten times double gain of happiness.   330
Go then, my mother, to thy daughter go,
Make bold her bashful years with your experience,
Prepare her ears to hear a wooer's tale,
Put in her tender heart the aspiring flame
Of golden sovereignty, acquaint the princess
With the sweet silent hours of marriage joys:
And when this arm of mine hath chastised
The petty rebel, dull-brain'd Buckingham,

Bound with triumphant garlands will I come,
And lead thy daughter to a conqueror's bed;   340
To whom I will retail my conquest won,
And she shall be sole victress, Cæsar's Cæsar.
Queen Eliz. What were I best to say? her father's brother
Would be her lord? or shall I say, her uncle?
Or, he that slew her brothers and her uncles?
Under what title shall I woo for thee,
That God, the law, my honour and her love,
Can make seem pleasing to her tender years?}
King Richard. Infer fair England's peace by this alliance.
Queen Eliz. Which she shall purchase with still lasting war.   350
King Richard. Say that the king, which may command, en-
    treats.
Queen Eliz. That at her hands which the king's King for-
    bids.
King Richard. Say, she shall be a high and mighty queen.
Queen Eliz. To wail the title, as her mother doth.
King Richard. Say, I will love her everlastingly.
Queen Eliz. But how long shall that title 'ever' last?
King Richard. Sweetly in force unto her fair life's end.
Queen Eliz. But how long fairly shall her sweet life last?
King Richard. So long as heaven and nature lengthens it.
Queen Eliz. So long as hell and Richard likes of it.   360
King Richard. Say, I, her sovereign, am her subject love.
Queen Eliz. But she, your subject, loathes such sovereignty.
King Richard. Be eloquent in my behalf to her.
Queen Eliz. An honest tale speeds best being plainly told.
King Richard. Then in plain terms tell her my loving tale.   †
Queen Eliz. Plain and not honest is too harsh a style.
King Richard. [Madam,] your reasons are too shallow and
    too quick.
Queen Eliz. O no, my reasons are too deep and dead;
    Too deep and dead, poor infants, in their grave.
King Richard. Harp not on that string, madam; that is past.   370
Queen Eliz. Harp on it still shall I till heart-strings break.
King Richard. Now, by my George, my garter, and my
    crown,—
Queen Eliz. Profan'd, dishonour'd, and the third usurp'd.

King Richard. I swear, by nothing—
Queen Eliz.   By nothing; for this is no oath:
   The George, profan'd, hath lost his holy honour;
   The garter, blemish'd, pawn'd his knightly virtue;
   The crown, usurp'd, disgrac'd his kingly dignity.
   If something thou wilt swear to be believ'd,
   Swear then by something that thou hast not wrong'd.
King Richard. Now, by the world—
Queen Eliz.   'Tis full of thy foul wrongs.   380
King Richard. My father's death—
Queen Eliz.   Thy life hath that dishonour'd.
King Richard. Then, by myself—
Queen Eliz.   Thyself thyself misusest.
King Richard. Why then, by God—
Queen Eliz.   God's wrong is most of all.
   If thou hadst fear'd to break an oath by Him,
   The unity the king thy brother made
   Had not been broken, nor my brother slain:
   If thou hadst fear'd to break an oath by Him,
   The imperial metal, circling now thy brow,
   Had grac'd the tender temples of my child,
   And both the princes had been breathing here,   390
   Which now, two tender playfellows for dust,
   Thy broken faith hath made a prey for worms.
   {What canst thou swear by now?}
King Richard.   [By] the time to come.
Queen Eliz. That thou hast wrong'd in time o'erpast;
   For I myself have many tears to wash
   Hereafter time, for time past wrong'd by thee.   †
   The children live, whose parents thou hast slaughter'd,
   Ungovern'd youth, to wail it in their age;
   The parents live, whose children thou hast butcher'd,
   Old wither'd plants, to wail it with their age.   400
   Swear not by time to come; for that thou hast
   Misus'd ere us'd, by time misus'd o'erpast.   †
King Richard. As I intend to prosper and repent,
   So thrive I in my dangerous attempt
   Of hostile arms, myself myself confound,
   Heaven and fortune bar me happy hours!

Day, yield me not thy light, nor, night, thy rest,
Be opposite, all planets of good luck,
To my proceedings, if, with pure heart's love,
Immaculate devotion, holy thoughts,   410
I tender not thy beauteous princely daughter!
In her consists my happiness and thine;
Without her, follows to this land and me,
To thee, herself, and many a Christian soul,
Sad desolation, ruin and decay:
It cannot be avoided but by this;
It will not be avoided but by this.
Therefore, good mother (I must call you so),
Be the attorney of my love to her:
Plead what I will be, not what I have been;   420
Not my deserts, but what I will deserve:
Urge the necessity and state of times,
And be not peevish-fond in great designs.
Queen Eliz. Shall I be tempted of the devil thus?
King Richard. Ay, if the devil tempt thee to do good.
Queen Eliz. Shall I forget myself to be myself?
King Richard. Ay, if your self's remembrance wrong your-
    self.
Queen Eliz. But thou didst kill my children.
King Richard. But in your daughter's womb I buried them: †
    Where in that nest of spicery they shall breed   430
    Selves of themselves, to your recomforture.
Queen Eliz. Shall I go win my daughter to thy will?
King Richard. And be a happy mother by the deed.
Queen Eliz. I go. Write to me very shortly,
    {And you shall understand from me her mind.}
King Richard. Bear her my true love's kiss; {and so,} fare-
    well.   *Exit Queen Elizabeth*
    Relenting fool, and shallow, changing woman!

Enter Ratcliff; Catesby following

{How now! what news?}
Ratcliff. My gracious sovereign, on the western coast
    Rideth a puissant navy; to the shore   440
    Throng many doubtful hollow-hearted friends,

Unarm'd, and unresolv'd to beat them back:
'Tis thought that Richmond is their admiral,
And there they hull, expecting but the aid
Of Buckingham to welcome them ashore.

King Richard. Some light-foot friend post to the Duke of
     Norfolk:
Ratcliff, thyself, or Catesby; where is he?

Catesby. Here, my lord.

King Richard. Fly to the duke. (*to Ratcliff*) Post thou to
     Salisbury:
When thou com'st there,— (*to Catesby*) Dull unmindful
     villain,   450
Why stand'st thou still, and go'st not to the duke?

Catesby. First, mighty sovereign, let me know your mind,
What from your grace I shall deliver them.

King Richard. O, true, good Catesby: bid him levy straight
The greatest strength and power he can make,
And meet me presently at Salisbury.

Catesby. I go.   *Exit*

Ratcliff. What is 't your highness' pleasure I shall do
At Salisbury?

King Richard. Why, what wouldst thou do there before I go? 460

Ratcliff. Your highness told me I should post before.

King Richard. My mind is chang'd, [sir, my mind is
     chang'd.]

Enter the Earl of Derby

How now, what news with you?

Derby. None good, my lord, to please you with the hearing;
Nor none so bad, but it may well be told.

King Richard. Hoyday, a riddle, neither good nor bad!
Why dost thou run so many mile about,
When thou mayst tell thy tale a nearer way?
Once more, what news?

Derby.   Richmond is on the seas.

King Richard. There let him sink, and be the seas on him!   470
White-liver'd runagate, what doth he there?

Derby. I know not, mighty sovereign, but by guess.

King Richard. Well, [sir, as you guess,] as you guess?

Derby. Stirr'd up by Dorset, Buckingham, and Ely,
  He makes for England, there to claim the crown.
King Richard. Is the chair empty? is the sword unsway'd?
  Is the king dead? the empire unpossess'd?
  What heir of York is there alive but we?
  And who is England's king but great York's heir?
  Then, tell me, what doth he upon the sea?   480
Derby. Unless for that, my liege, I cannot guess.
King Richard. Unless for that he comes to be your liege,
  You cannot guess wherefore the Welshman comes.
  Thou wilt revolt and fly to him, I fear.
Derby. No, mighty liege; therefore mistrust me not.
King Richard. Where is thy power then? to beat him back,
  Where are thy tenants? and thy followers?
  Are they not now upon the western shore,
  Safe-conducting the rebels from their ships?
Derby. No, my good lord, my friends are in the north.   490
King Richard. Cold friends to Richard, what do they in the
      north,
  When they should serve their sovereign in the west?
Derby. They have not been commanded, mighty sovereign:
  Please it your majesty to give me leave,
  I'll muster up my friends, and meet your grace
  Where and what time your majesty shall please.
King Richard. Ay, [ay,] thou wouldst be gone to join with
      Richmond:
  I will not trust you, sir.
Derby.   Most mighty sovereign,
  You have no cause to hold my friendship doubtful:
  I never was nor never will be false.   500
King Richard. Well,
  Go muster men, but, hear you, leave behind
  Your son, George Stanley: look your faith be firm,
  Or else his head's assurance is but frail.
Derby. So deal with him as I prove true to you.   *Exit*

Enter a Messenger

Messenger. My gracious sovereign, now in Devonshire,
  As I by friends am well advertised,

Sir William Courtney, and the haughty prelate,
Bishop of Exeter, his brother there,
With many moe confederates, are in arms.   510

Enter another Messenger

Sec. Mess. My liege, in Kent, the Guildfords are in arms,
And every hour more competitors
Flock to their aid, and still their power increaseth.

Enter another Messenger

Third Mess. My lord, the army of the Duke of Bucking-
ham—
King Richard. Out on you, owls! nothing but songs of death!
                                    He striketh him
Take that, until thou bring me better news.
Third Mess. Your grace mistakes; the news I bring is good,
My news is that by sudden flood, and fall of water,
The Duke of Buckingham's army is dispers'd and scatter'd,
And he himself fled, no man knows whither.   520
King Richard. O, I cry you mercy, I did mistake;
Ratcliff, reward him for the blow I gave him.
Hath any well-advised friend given out
Rewards for him that brings in Buckingham?
Third Mess. Such proclamation hath been made, my liege.

Enter another Messenger

Fourth Mess. Sir Thomas Lovel and Lord Marquis Dorset,
'Tis said, my liege, are up in arms.
Yet this good comfort bring I to your grace,
The Breton navy is dispers'd {by tempest}:
Richmond, in Dorsetshire,   530
Sent out a boat to ask them on the shore
If they were his assistants, yea or no;
Who answer'd him, they came from Buckingham
Upon his party: he, mistrusting them,
Hois'd sail, and made away for Brittany.
King Richard. March on, march on, since we are up in arms;
If not to fight with foreign enemies,
Yet to beat down these rebels here at home.

Re-enter Catesby

Catesby. My liege, the Duke of Buckingham is taken;
   That is the best news: that the Earl of Richmond   540
   Is with a mighty power landed at Milford,
   Is colder tidings, yet they must be told.
King Richard. Away towards Salisbury! while we reason
   here,
   A royal battle might be won and lost,
   Some one take order Buckingham be brought
   To Salisbury, the rest march on with me.

                       Flourish. Exeunt

SCENE V

Lord Derby's house

Enter Derby and Sir Christopher Urswick

Derby. Sir Christopher, tell Richmond this from me:
   That in the sty of this most bloody boar
   My son George Stanley is frank'd up in hold:
   If I revolt, off goes young George's head;
   The fear of that withholds my present aid.
   {So, get thee gone; commend me to thy lord;
   Withal say that the queen hath heartily consented
   He should espouse Elizabeth her daughter.}
   But, tell me, where is princely Richmond now?
Urswick. At Pembroke, or at Ha'rford-west, in Wales.   10
Derby. What men of name resort to him?
Urswick. Sir Walter Herbert, a renowned soldier,
   Sir Gilbert Talbot, Sir William Stanley,
   Oxford, redoubted Pembroke, Sir James Blunt,
   And Rice ap Thomas, with a valiant crew,
   And many moe of noble fame and worth:
   And towards London they do bend their course,
   If by the way they be not fought withal.
Derby. Return unto thy lord, commend me to him,
   [Tell him the queen hath heartily consented   20

He shall espouse Elizabeth her daughter.]
These letters will resolve him of my mind.
Farewell.   *Exeunt*

Act Fifth

Salisbury. An open place

*Enter [Ratcliff] {the Sheriff}, and Buckingham, with
halberds, led to execution*

Buckingham. Will not King Richard let me speak with him?
Ratcliff. No, my {good} lord; therefore be patient.
Buckingham. Hastings, and Edward's children, Rivers, Grey,
Holy King Henry, and thy fair son Edward,
Vaughan, and all that have miscarried
By underhand corrupted foul injustice,
If that your moody discontented souls
Do through the clouds behold this present hour,
Even for revenge mock my destruction!
This is All-Souls' day, fellows, is it not?   10
Ratcliff. It is, [my lord.]
Buckingham. Why, then All-Souls' day is my body's dooms-
day.
This is the day that, in King Edward's time,
I wish'd might fall on me, when I was found
False to his children or his wife's allies;
This is the day wherein I wish'd to fall
By the false faith of him I trusted most;
This, this All-Souls' day to my fearful soul
Is the determin'd respite of my wrongs:
That high All-seer that I dallied with   20
Hath turn'd my feigned prayer on my head,
And given in earnest what I begg'd in jest.
Thus doth he force the swords of wicked men

95

To turn their own points on their masters' bosoms;
Now Margaret's curse is fallen upon my head;
'When he,' quoth she, 'shall split thy heart with sorrow,
Remember Margaret was a prophetess.'
Come, sirs, convey me to the block of shame;
Wrong hath but wrong, and blame the due of blame.

Exeunt

SCENE II

The camp near Tamworth

*Enter Richmond, {Oxford, Blunt, Herbert,} and others,
with drum and trumpets*

Richmond. Fellows in arms, and my most loving friends,
  Bruis'd underneath the yoke of tyranny,
  Thus far into the bowels of the land
  Have we march'd on without impediment,
  And here receive we, from our father Stanley,
  Lines of fair comfort and encouragement.
  The wretched, bloody, and usurping boar,
  That spoil'd your summer fields and fruitful vines,
  Swills your warm blood like wash, and makes his trough
  In your embowell'd bosoms, this foul swine   10
  Lies now even in the centre of this isle,
  Near to the town of Leicester, as we learn:
  From Tamworth thither is but one day's march;
  In God's name, cheerly on, courageous friends,
  To reap the harvest of perpetual peace
  By this one bloody trial of sharp war.
First Lord. Every man's conscience is a thousand swords,
  To fight against that bloody homicide.
Sec. Lord. I doubt not but his friends will fly to us.
Third Lord. He hath no friends but who are friends for fear, 20
  Which in his greatest need will shrink from him.
Richmond. All for our vantage; then, in God's name, march:
  True hope is swift, and flies with swallow's wings,
  Kings it makes gods, and meaner creatures kings.

Exeunt

SCENE III

Bosworth Field

Enter King Richard in arms with Norfolk, Ratcliff,
[Catesby], {the Earl of Surrey}, and others   †

King Richard. Here pitch our tents, even here in Bosworth
   field.
   Why, how now, Catesby, why look'st thou so sad?
Catesby. My heart is ten times lighter than my looks.
King Richard. Norfolk, come hither.
{Norfolk.   Here, most gracious liege.
King Richard.} Norfolk, we must have knocks; ha! must we
   not?
Norfolk. We must both give and take, my gracious lord.
King Richard. Up with my tent [there!] here will I lie to-
   night:
   But where to-morrow—well, all's one for that.
   Who hath descried the number of the foe?
Norfolk. Six or seven thousand is their greatest number.   10
King Richard. Why, our battalion trebles that account:
   Besides, the king's name is a tower of strength,
   Which they upon the adverse party want.
   Up with my tent there! Valiant gentlemen,
   Let us survey the vantage of the field,
   Call for some men of sound direction,
   Let's want no discipline, make no delay,
   For, lords, to-morrow is a busy day.   *Exeunt*

Enter, on the other side of the field, Richmond, Sir William
Brandon, Oxford, Herbert, Blunt, and others. Some of the Sol-
diers pitch Richmond's tent

Richmond. The weary sun hath made a golden set,
   And by the bright track of his fiery car   20
   Gives signal of a goodly day to-morrow.
   Where is Sir William Brandon, he shall bear my stand-
   ard.

{Give me some ink and paper in my tent;
I'll draw the form and model of our battle,
Limit each leader to his several charge,
And part in just proportion our small strength.
My Lord of Oxford, you, Sir William Brandon,
And you, Sir Walter Herbert, stay with me.}
The Earl of Pembroke keeps his regiment:
Good Captain Blunt, bear my good-night to him, 30
And by the second hour in the morning
Desire the earl to see me in my tent:
Yet one thing more, good Blunt, before thou go'st,
Where is Lord Stanley quarter'd, dost thou know?
Blunt. Unless I have mista'en his colours much,
Which well I am assur'd I have not done,
His regiment lies half a mile at least
South from the mighty power of the king.
Richmond. If without peril it be possible,
Good Captain Blunt, bear my good-night to him, 40
And give him from me this most needful scroll.
Blunt. Upon my life, my lord, I'll undertake it;
{And so, God give you quiet rest to-night!}
Richmond. Farewell, good Blunt.
[Give me some ink and paper in my tent;
I'll draw the form and model of our battle,
Limit each leader to his several charge,
And part in just proportion our small strength.]
Come, let us consult upon to-morrow's business:
In to our tent! the air is raw and cold. 50

They withdraw into the tent

*Enter, to his tent, King Richard, Norfolk, Ratcliff,
Catesby, and others*

King Richard. What is 't o'clock?
Catesby. It is six o'clock, full supper-time;
King Richard. I will not sup to-night. Give me some ink and
paper.
What, is my beaver easier than it was!
And all my armour laid into my tent?
Catesby. It is, my liege; and all things are in readiness.

King Richard. Good Norfolk, hie thee to thy charge;
 Use careful watch, choose trusty sentinels.
Norfolk. I go, my lord.
King Richard. Stir with the lark to-morrow, gentle Norfolk. 60
Norfolk. I warrant you, my lord.   *Exit*
King Richard. Catesby!
Catesby. My lord?
King Richard. Send out a pursuivant at arms
 To Stanley's regiment; bid him bring his power
 Before sunrising, lest his son George fall
 Into the blind cave of eternal night. *Exit Catesby*
 Fill me a bowl of wine. Give me a watch.
 Saddle white Surrey for the field to-morrow.
 Look that my staves be sound, and not too heavy.
 Ratcliff!   70
Ratcliff. My lord?
King Richard. Saw'st thou the melancholy Lord Northum-
  berland?
Ratcliff. Thomas the Earl of Surrey, and himself,
 Much about cock-shut time, from troop to troop
 Went through the army, cheering up the soldiers.
King Richard. So, I am satisfied. Give me a bowl of wine:
 I have not that alacrity of spirit,
 Nor cheer of mind, that I was wont to have.
 Set it down. Is ink and paper ready?
Ratcliff.   It is, my lord.
King Richard. Bid my guard watch. Leave me. Ratcliff, 80
 About the mid of night come to my tent,
 And help to arm me. Leave me, I say.
    Exeunt Ratcliff and the other attendants

  Enter Derby to Richmond in his tent, Lords and others
       attending

Derby. Fortune and victory sit on thy helm!
Richmond. All comfort that the dark night can afford
 Be to thy person, noble father-in-law!
 Tell me, how fares our loving mother?
Derby. I, by attorney, bless thee from thy mother,
 Who prays continually for Richmond's good:

So much for that. The silent hours steal on,
And flaky darkness breaks within the east.   90
In brief, for so the season bids us be,
Prepare thy battle early in the morning,
And put thy fortune to the arbitrement
Of bloody strokes and mortal-staring war.
I, as I may—that which I would I cannot,—
With best advantage will deceive the time,
And aid thee in this doubtful shock of arms:
But on thy side I may not be too forward,
Lest, being seen, thy brother, tender George,
Be executed in his father's sight.   100
Farewell: the leisure and the fearful time
Cuts off the ceremonious vows of love,
And ample interchange of sweet discourse,
Which so long sunder'd friends should dwell upon:
God give us leisure for these rites of love!
Once more, adieu: be valiant, and speed well!
Richmond. Good lords, conduct him to his regiment:
  I'll strive with troubled thoughts to take a nap,
  Lest leaden slumber peise me down to-morrow,
  When I should mount with wings of victory: 110
  Once more, good night, kind lords and gentlemen.

                              Exeunt all but Richmond

O Thou, whose captain I account myself,
Look on my forces with a gracious eye;
Put in their hands thy bruising irons of wrath,
That they may crush down with a heavy fall
The usurping helmets of our adversaries!
Make us thy ministers of chastisement,
That we may praise thee in the victory!
To thee I do commend my watchful soul,
Ere I let fall the windows of mine eyes: 120
Sleeping and waking, O, defend me still!   *Sleeps*

  Enter the Ghost of Prince Edward, son to Henry the Sixth

Ghost. (*to Richard*) Let me sit heavy on thy soul to-
  morrow!

Think, how thou stab'dst me in my prime of youth
At Tewkesbury: despair, therefore, and die!
(*to Richmond*) Be cheerful, Richmond; for the wronged
   souls
Of butcher'd princes fight in thy behalf:
King Henry's issue, Richmond, comforts thee.

Enter the Ghost of Henry the Sixth

Ghost. (*to Richard*) When I was mortal, my anointed body
   By thee was punched full of [deadly] holes:
   Think on the Tower and me: despair, and die!   130
   Harry the Sixth bids thee despair, and die!
   (*to Richmond*) Virtuous and holy, be thou conqueror!
   Harry, that prophesied thou shouldst be king,
   Doth comfort thee in thy sleep: live, and flourish!

Enter the Ghost of Clarence

Ghost. (*to Richard*) Let me sit heavy in thy soul to-morrow!
   I, that was wash'd to death with fulsome wine,
   Poor Clarence, by thy guile betray'd to death.
   To-morrow in the battle think on me,
   And fall thy edgeless sword: despair, and die!
   (*to Richmond*) Thou offspring of the house of Lancas-
      ter,   140
   The wronged heirs of York do pray for thee:
   Good angels guard thy battle! live, and flourish!

Enter the Ghosts of Rivers, Grey, and Vaughan

Ghost. (*to Richard*) Let me sit heavy in thy soul to-morrow,
   Rivers, that died at Pomfret! despair, and die!
Ghost. (*to Richard*) Think upon Grey, and let thy soul
      despair!
Ghost. (*to Richard*) Think upon Vaughan, and, with guilty
      fear,
   Let fall thy lance: despair, and die!
All. (*to Richmond*) Awake, and think our wrongs in Rich-
      ard's bosom
   Will conquer him! awake, and win the day!

Enter the Ghosts of the two young Princes

Ghost. (*to Richard*) Dream on thy cousins smother'd in
    the Tower: 150
  Let us be lead within thy bosom, Richard,
  And weigh thee down to ruin, shame, and death!
  Thy nephews' souls bid thee despair and die!
  (*to Richmond*) Sleep, Richmond, sleep in peace, and
    wake in joy;
  Good angels guard thee from the boar's annoy!
  Live, and beget a happy race of kings!
  Edward's unhappy sons do bid thee flourish.

Enter the Ghost of Hastings

Ghost. (*to Richard*) Bloody and guilty, guiltily awake,
  And in a bloody battle end thy days!
  Think on Lord Hastings: despair, and die!   160
  (*to Richmond*) Quiet untroubled soul, awake, awake!
  Arm, fight, and conquer, for fair England's sake!

Enter the Ghost of Lady Anne his wife

Ghost. (*to Richard*) Richard, thy wife, that wretched Anne
    thy wife,
  That never slept a quiet hour with thee,
  Now fills thy sleep with perturbations:
  To-morrow in the battle think on me,
  And fall thy edgeless sword: despair, and die!
  (*to Richmond*) Thou quiet soul, sleep thou a quiet sleep:
  Dream of success and happy victory!
  Thy adversary's wife doth pray for thee.   170

Enter the Ghost of Buckingham

Ghost. (*to Richard*) The first was I that help'd thee to the
    crown,
  The last was I that felt thy tyranny:
  O, in the battle think on Buckingham,
  And die in terror of thy guiltiness!
  Dream on, dream on, of bloody deeds and death:
  Fainting, despair; despairing, yield thy breath!
  (*to Richmond*) I died for hope ere I could lend thee aid:

But cheer thy heart, and be thou not dismay'd:
God and good angels fight on Richmond's side;
And Richard falls in height of all his pride.   180

     The Ghosts vanish. King Richard starts
           out of his dream

King Richard. Give me another horse, bind up my wounds,
Have mercy, Jesu!—Soft! I did but dream.
O coward conscience, how dost thou afflict me!
The lights burn blue, it is now dead midnight.
Cold fearful drops stand on my trembling flesh;
What do I fear? myself? there's none else by:
Richard loves Richard; that is I and I.
Is there a murderer here? No. Yes, I am:
Then fly. What, from myself? Great reason why:
Lest I revenge. What, myself upon myself?   190
Alack, I love myself. Wherefore? for any good
That I myself have done unto myself?
O, no! alas, I rather hate myself
For hateful deeds committed by myself!
I am a villain: yet I lie, I am not.
Fool, of thyself speak well: fool, do not flatter.
My conscience hath a thousand several tongues,
And every tongue brings in a several tale,
And every tale condemns me for a villain.
Perjury, [perjury,] in the high'st degree;   200
Murder, stern murder, in the direst degree;
All several sins, all us'd in each degree,
Throng to the bar, crying all 'Guilty! guilty!'
I shall despair; there is no creature loves me,
And if I die, no soul will pity me:
Nay, wherefore should they, since that I myself
Find in myself no pity to myself?
Methought the souls of all that I had murder'd
Came to my tent, and every one did threat
To-morrow's vengeance on the head of Richard.   210

       Enter Ratcliff

Ratcliff. My lord!
King Richard. ['Zounds!] who is there!

Ratcliff. Ratcliff, my lord; 'tis I. The early village-cock
Hath twice done salutation to the morn;
Your friends are up, and buckle on their armour.
[*King Richard.* O Ratcliff, I have dream'd a fearful dream!
What thinkest thou, will our friends prove all true?
Ratcliff. No doubt, my lord.]
King Richard.   O Ratcliff, I fear, I fear,—
Ratcliff. Nay, good my lord, be not afraid of shadows.
King Richard. By the apostle Paul, shadows to-night   220
Have struck more terror to the soul of Richard,
Than can the substance of ten thousand soldiers,
Armed in proof, and led by shallow Richmond.
It is not yet near day. Come, go with me;
Under our tents I'll play the eaves-dropper,
To see if any mean to shrink from me.   *Exeunt*

Enter the Lords to Richmond, sitting in his tent

Lords. Good morrow, Richmond!
Richmond. Cry mercy, lords and watchful gentlemen,
That you have ta'en a tardy sluggard here.
Lords. How have you slept, my lord?   230
Richmond. The sweetest sleep, and fairest-boding dreams
That ever enter'd in a drowsy head,
Have I since your departure had, my lords.
Methought their souls, whose bodies Richard murder'd,
Came to my tent, and cried on victory:
I promise you, my soul is very jocund,
In the remembrance of so fair a dream.
How far into the morning is it, lords?
Lords. Upon the stroke of four.
Richmond. Why, then 'tis time to arm and give direction.   240
            HIS ORATION TO HIS SOLDIERS   †
More than I have said, loving countrymen,
The leisure and enforcement of the time
Forbids to dwell upon; yet remember this,
God, and our good cause, fight upon our side;
The prayers of holy saints and wronged souls,
Like high-rear'd bulwarks, stand before our faces;
Richard except, those whom we fight against

Had rather have us win than him they follow:
For what is he they follow? truly, gentlemen,
A bloody tyrant, and a homicide;   250
One rais'd in blood, and one in blood establish'd;
One that made means to come by what he hath,
And slaughter'd those that were the means to help him;
A base foul stone, made precious by the foil
Of England's chair, where he is falsely set;
One that hath ever been God's enemy:
Then, if you fight against God's enemy,
God will in justice ward you as his soldiers;
If you do sweat to put a tyrant down,
You sleep in peace, the tyrant being slain;   260
If you do fight against your country's foes,
Your country's fat shall pay your pains the hire;
If you do fight in safeguard of your wives,
Your wives shall welcome home the conquerors;
If you do free your children from the sword,
Your children's children quits it in your age.
Then, in the name of God and all these rights,
Advance your standards, draw your willing swords.
For me, the ransom of my bold attempt
Shall be this cold corpse on the earth's cold face;   270
But if I thrive, the gain of my attempt
The least of you shall share his part thereof.
Sound drums and trumpets boldly and cheerfully;
God and Saint George! Richmond and victory!

Exeunt

Re-enter King Richard, Ratcliff, Attendants and Forces

King Richard. What said Northumberland, as touching Richmond?

Ratcliff. That he was never trained up in arms.

King Richard. He said the truth: and what said Surrey, then?

Ratcliff. He smil'd and said 'The better for our purpose.'

King Richard. He was in the right; and so indeed it is.

The clock striketh

Tell the clock there. Give me a calendar. 280
Who saw the sun to-day?
Ratcliff.   Not I, my lord.
King Richard. Then he disdains to shine, for by the book
He should have brav'd the east an hour ago:
A black day will it be to somebody.
Ratcliff!
Ratcliff. My lord?
King Richard.   The sun will not be seen to-day,
The sky doth frown, and lour upon our army;
I would these dewy tears were from the ground.
Not shine to-day! Why, what is that to me
More than to Richmond? for the selfsame heaven 290
That frowns on me looks sadly upon him.

Re-enter Norfolk

Norfolk. Arm, arm, my lord; the foe vaunts in the field.
King Richard. Come, bustle, bustle. Caparison my horse.
Call up Lord Stanley, bid him bring his power:
I will lead forth my soldiers to the plain,
And thus my battle shall be ordered:
My foreward shall be drawn out all in length,
Consisting equally of horse and foot;
Our archers shall be placed in the midst;
John Duke of Norfolk, Thomas Earl of Surrey, 300
Shall have the leading of this foot and horse.
They thus directed, we will follow
In the main battle, whose puissance on either side
Shall be well winged with our chiefest horse.
This, and Saint George to boot! What think'st thou, Nor-
folk?
Norfolk. A good direction, warlike sovereign.
This found I on my tent this morning.
He sheweth him a paper
King Richard. (*reads*) 'Jockey of Norfolk, be not so bold,
For Dickon thy master is bought and sold.'
A thing devised by the enemy. 310

Go, gentlemen, every man unto his charge:
Let not our babbling dreams affright our souls:
Conscience is but a word that cowards use,
Devis'd at first to keep the strong in awe:
Our strong arms be our conscience, swords our law.
March on, join bravely, let us to 't pell-mell;
If not to heaven, then hand in hand to hell.

HIS ORATION TO HIS ARMY

What shall I say more than I have inferr'd?
Remember whom you are to cope withal,
A sort of vagabonds, rascals, and runaways,   320
A scum of Bretons, and base lackey peasants,
Whom their o'er-cloyed country vomits forth,
To desperate adventures and assur'd destruction.
You sleeping safe, they bring to you unrest;
You having lands and blest with beauteous wives,
They would restrain the one, distain the other.
And who doth lead them but a paltry fellow?
Long kept in Brittany at our mother's cost,
A milk-sop, one that never in his life
Felt so much cold as over shoes in snow.   330
Let's whip these stragglers o'er the seas again,
Lash hence these overweening rags of France,
These famish'd beggars, weary of their lives,
Who, but for dreaming on this fond exploit,
For want of means, poor rats, had hang'd themselves:
If we be conquer'd, let men conquer us,
And not these bastard Bretons, whom our fathers
Have in their own land beaten, bobb'd, and thump'd,
And in record left them the heirs of shame.
Shall these enjoy our lands? lie with our wives?   340
Ravish our daughters? (*Drum afar off.*) Hark! I hear
   their drum.
Fight, gentlemen of England! fight, bold yeomen!
Draw, archers, draw your arrows to the head!
Spur your proud horses hard, and ride in blood;
Amaze the welkin with your broken staves!

Enter a Messenger

What says Lord Stanley? will he bring his power?
Messenger. My lord, he doth deny to come.
King Richard. Off with his son George's head!
Norfolk. My lord, the enemy is past the marsh,
    After the battle let George Stanley die.   350
King Richard. A thousand hearts are great within my
    bosom:
    Advance our standards, set upon our foes;
    Our ancient word of courage, fair Saint George,
    Inspire us with the spleen of fiery dragons!
    Upon them! Victory sits on our helms.   *Exeunt*

SCENES IV AND V

The field of battle

Alarum: excursions. Enter Catesby   †

Catesby. Rescue, my Lord of Norfolk, rescue, rescue!
    The king enacts more wonders than a man,
    Daring an opposite to every danger:
    His horse is slain, and all on foot he fights,
    Seeking for Richmond in the throat of death.
    Rescue, fair lord, or else the day is lost!

Alarums. Enter King Richard

King Richard. A horse! a horse! my kingdom for a horse!
Catesby. Withdraw, my lord; I'll help you to a horse.
King Richard. Slave, I have set my life upon a cast,
    And I will stand the hazard of the die.   10
    I think there be six Richmonds in the field;
    Five have I slain to-day instead of him.
    A horse! a horse! my kingdom for a horse!   *Exeunt*

Alarum. Enter Richard and Richmond; they fight.
Richard is slain

Retreat and flourish

Re-enter Richmond, Derby bearing the crown, with divers
other Lords

Richmond. God and your arms be prais'd, victorious friends!
   The day is ours, the bloody dog is dead.
Derby. Courageous Richmond, well hast thou acquit thee.
   Lo, here, this long usurped royalty
   From the dead temples of this bloody wretch
   Have I pluck'd off, to grace thy brows withal:
   Wear it, [enjoy it,] and make much of it.
Richmond. Great God of heaven, say amen to all!
   But, tell me, is young George Stanley living?
Derby. He is, my lord, and safe in Leicester town;   10
   Whither, if it please you, we may now withdraw us.
Richmond. What men of name are slain on either side?
Derby. John Duke of Norfolk, Walter Lord Ferrers,
   Sir Robert Brakenbury, and Sir William Brandon.
Richmond. Inter their bodies as becomes their births:
   Proclaim a pardon to the soldiers fled,
   That in submission will return to us:
   And then, as we have ta'en the sacrament,
   We will unite the white rose and the red.
   Smile heaven upon this fair conjunction,   20
   That long have frown'd upon their enmity!
   What traitor hears me, and says not amen?
   England hath long been mad, and scarr'd herself;
   The brother blindly shed the brother's blood,
   The father rashly slaughter'd his own son,
   The son, compell'd, been butcher to the sire:
   All this divided York and Lancaster,
   Divided in their dire division.
   O, now let Richmond and Elizabeth,

The true succeeders of each royal house,   30
By God's fair ordinance conjoin together,
And let their heirs, God, if thy will be so,
Enrich the time to come with smooth-fac'd peace,
With smiling plenty and fair prosperous days!
Abate the edge of traitors, gracious Lord,
That would reduce these bloody days again,
And make poor England weep in streams of blood!
Let them not live to taste this land's increase,
That would with treason wound this fair land's peace!
Now civil wounds are stopp'd, peace lives again: 40
That she may long live here, God say amen!   *Exeunt*

Notes

Three pairs of passages are appended, which may serve to illustrate the frequent unimportant differences between the Q and F texts.

(*a*) I. iv. 274–77.

> Now must I *hide* his *body in some hole,*
> Until *the duke* take *order for his burial:*
> *And when I have my meed* I must *away,*
> *For this will out, and* here *I must not stay.*   (Q)

> Well, I'll go *hide* the *body in some hole,*
> Till that *the duke* give *order for his burial:*
> *And when I have my meed,* I will *away,*
> *For this will out, and* then *I must not stay.*   (F)

(*b*) III. vi. 8–14.

> *And yet within these five hours* liv'd Lord Hastings,
> *Untainted, unexamined, free, at liberty:*
> *Here's a good world, the while.* Why who's *so gross*
> *That* sees not *this palpable device?*
> *Yet who's so* blind *but says he sees it not?*
> *Bad is the world, and all will come to nought,*
> *When such* bad *dealing must be seen in thought.*   (Q)

> *And yet within these five hours* Hastings liv'd,
> *Untainted, unexamin'd, free, at liberty.*
> *Here's a good world the while.*
> Who is *so gross, that* cannot see *this palpable device?*
> *Yet who so* bold, *but says he sees it not?*

111

> *Bad is the world, and all will come to nought,*
> *When such* ill *dealing must be seen in thought.*   (F)

(*c*) IV. iii. 1–11.

> *The tyrannous and bloody* deed *is done,*
> *The most arch* act *of piteous massacre,*
> *That ever yet this land was guilty of,*
> *Dighton and Forrest whom I did suborn,*
> *To do this* ruthless piece of butchery,
> Although *they were flesh'd villains, bloody dogs,*
> Melting *with tenderness and* kind *compassion,*
> *Wept like* two *children in their deaths' sad* stories:
> *Lo* thus quoth Dighton lay *those tender babes,*
> *Thus thus quoth Forrest girdling one another,*
> *Within their* innocent alabaster *arms.*   (Q)

> *The tyrannous and bloody* act *is done,*
> *The most arch* deed *of piteous massacre*
> *That ever yet this land was guilty of:*
> *Dighton and Forrest,* who *I did suborn*
> *To do this* piece of ruthful butchery,
> Albeit *they were flesh'd villains, bloody dogs,*
> Melted *with tenderness, and* mild *compassion,*
> *Wept like* to *children, in their deaths' sad* story.
> *O* thus (*quoth Dighton*) lay *the gentle babes:*
> *Thus, thus* (*quoth Forrest*) *girdling one another*
> *Within their* alabaster innocent *arms.*   (F).

I. i. 13. *pleasing of a love*; so Q, F reads *lute*. Neither reading is very satisfactory, and *pleasing* is in any case difficult: but *lute* seems to make the picture needlessly ridiculous, and less consonant with the *To strut before a wanton ambling nymph* of four lines lower.

I. i. 65. *That tempers him to this extremity*; so Q 1. The later Qq read either *tempts* or *temps*, and the Folio, conducting, one can hardly doubt, the same operation as produced the famous 'haughty Scot' line in 2 *Henry IV*, reads *That tempts him to this harsh extremity*.

I. i. 73. *Mistress Shore*; she was the wife of a Lombard Street goldsmith. Whether or not she was the King's mistress, as is frequently implied in the play, she had certainly undue influence over him.

I. ii. 19. *to adders, spiders, toads*; so Q. F has the mysterious alteration *to wolves, to spiders, toads*, less balanced, and less apposite.

I. ii. 37. *Cf.* Hamlet's *By Heaven, I'll make a ghost of him that lets me.*

I. ii. 89. *Why then they are not dead*; so Q. F has the less pointed *Then say they were not slain.*

I. ii. 94. *bloody falchion*; so Q. F reads *murd'rous falchion*, so avoiding repetition.

I. ii. 124. *rest one hour*; so Q. F reads *live one hour*, providing a contrast with *death* in the line before, which compensates for the loss of vividness.

I. ii. 226. Gloucester's order, which F omits, seems essential.

I. iii. 41–2. (S.D.); Hastings and Dorset are not included in the stage-direction by either Q or F, and it is arguable that Gloucester's entry is more effective alone. It is true, however, that though the other two are not needed for 130 lines, there is no other point which gives them an effective entry.

I. iii. 61. *lewd*; so both Q and F. But (?) *loud*.

I. iii. 68. *Makes him to send . . . remove it*; instead of these two lines F has only one, *Makes him to send, that he may learn the ground.*

I. iii. 125. *spilt*; so Q. F *spent.*

I. iii. 175. *crown his warlike brows with paper*; see 3 *Henry VI,* I. iv.

I. iii. 265. *scorns the sun*; editors seem happy enough about this phrase, but I cannot feel that it is very satisfactory, nor that it well introduces Margaret's retort. *Fronts,* or some such word, would seem nearer to the required sense.

I. iii. 291. *venom'd*; Q and F *venome*; but the *e:d* confusion is common, and though no doubt *venom* may stand, it seems reasonable to make the change. Q 1 then reads *rackle thee to death,* Q 2–6 *rankle thee to death,* F *rankle to the death. Rackle* is only known once as a verb, and even then not in the required sense; but *rankle* is common enough transitively, so that we need not follow F in transposing the order.

I. iii. 349. *May move your hearts to pity*; Q reads *May, move your hearts* . . . This illustrates the perils and seductions of attention to Elizabethan punctuation. I am surprised that it has not been adduced as an example of subtlety, as indeed it might; Gloucester pauses after *May* and has another glance at his two villains, and then continues with an ironic smile. On the other hand the comma may simply have found its way in by error for a space.

I. iv. 1. (S.D. and speech-headings). F gives *Keeper* down to line 74, after which *Enter Brakenbury* and opens his speech with *Sorrow breaks*. A fairly clear case of Q economising an actor.

I. iv. 9. *Methoughts . . . Burgundy*; F expands to (or Q was contracted from) two lines:

> *Methoughts that I had broken from the Tower,*
> *And was embark'd to cross to Burgundy.*

I. iv. 38. *empty vast and wandering air*; so Q. F inserts a comma after *empty*, making *vast* an adjective instead of the emphatic noun.

I. iv. 81. *low names*; so Q. F reads *name* to produce a couplet. But the plural *names* is badly wanted, and a better emendation for rhyme would have been *fames*.

In the rest of the scene there are considerable divergences between Q and F, of which only a few can easily be indicated.

I. iv. 113. *my holy humour*; so Q. *This passionate humour of mine*, F.

I. iv. 143. *strong in fraud*; so Q. F reads *strong fram'd*, a tempting but not imperative emendation.

I. iv. 146. *shall we to this gear*; so Q. F reads *shall we fall to work*.

I. iv. 181. *to have redemption . . . sins*; so Q. F omits the second line altogether, and reads *for any goodness* instead of *to have redemption*.

I. iv. 195–96. F tidies up the metre thus:

> *Thou didst receive the sacrament to fight*
> *In quarrel of the house of Lancaster.*

I. iv. 217–18. F reads:

> *Thy brother's love, our duty, and thy fault*
> *Provoke us hither now to slaughter thee.*

and in l. 237:

> *'Tis he that sends us to destroy you here.*

I. iv. 250–61. F, besides having 7 lines which are not in Q, has a quite different order, thus:

Clar. *Relent, and save your souls.*
  Which of you, if you were a prince's son,
  Being pent from liberty, as I am now,
  If two such murderers as yourselves came to you,
  Would not entreat for life as you would beg
  Were you in my distress.
1.M. *Relent! no, 'tis cowardly and womanish.*
Clar. *Not to relent is beastly, savage, devilish.*
  My friend, I spy some pity in thy looks;
  O, if thine eye be not a flatterer,
  Come thou on my side and entreat for me;
  A begging prince what beggar pities not?

This is clearly awkward, though not wholly impossible. This passage tells strongly against the supposition that F was printed from the original MS., neglecting the cuts, and for the supposition that it was printed either from a Quarto which had had the insertions clumsily made, or from a MS. (possibly with an intervening transcript) which had had the insertions equally clumsily made. But it is of course quite possible that the insertions themselves were taken from the original MS., though I cannot help feeling that the passage is more vigorous without them, and that they are somewhat suspect.

I. iv. 263–64. F makes this tidy and ordinary and metrical:

> *Take that, and that: if all this will not do,*
> *I'll drown you in the malmsey-butt within.*

II. i. 7. *Rivers and Hastings*; so Q. F gets in a muddle, reading *Dorset and Rivers*, but leaving the succeeding speech-headings as in Q (i.e. *Rivers* and *Hastings*) and not introducing Dorset till l. 26, with the somewhat awkward extra l. 25.

II. i. 45. *here comes the noble duke*; so Q. The F reading is an oddity:

> And in good time
> Here comes Sir Richard Ratcliff and the duke.

followed by stage-direction *Enter Ratcliff and Gloster*. Since Ratcliff says and does nothing in the rest of the scene, his metrically awkward introduction seems quite pointless.

II. i. 66, 68. Here there is more trouble with proper names. Instead of Rivers and Grey in l. 66 F has Rivers and Dorset; and it then inserts a line in which the titles, if they refer to anyone, can only refer to Rivers, whose name (not title) was Woodvill, and whose style, till he succeeded to the earldom, was Scales. It looks as though marginal notes, or preliminary attempts, had found their way into print.

II. i. 98–108. Here is one of the 'blocks' of minor alterations: for the *grant* (98), *speak* and *demand'st* (99), *the same* (104), *slew* (105), *cruel* (106), *rage* (107), and *bade* (108), of Q, F reads: *hear me, say* and *requests, that tongue, kill'd, bitter, wrath,* and *bid*, besides reading a meaningless *and* for *at* in 108.

II. ii. 23–4. This passage should be compared with I. iv. 238–39. Both are as in Q. F reads for the earlier:

> It cannot be; for he bewept my fortune,
> And hugg'd me in his arms, and swore with sobs . . .

and for the second:

> And when my uncle told me so, he wept
> And pitied me, and kindly kiss'd my cheek.

II. ii. 33. (S.D.); the omission by Q of Rivers and Dorset from the stage-direction and later in the scene (89–100, and 123–40) looks unmistakably like cutting.

II. ii. 46. *perpetual rest*; so Q. F has the reading, which seems curiously inappropriate to the context and the Queen's sentiments, *ne'er-changing night*.

II. ii. 127. *green*; this word, standing where it does, is an interesting example of the way in which Shakespeare's imagination often works. The word means 'raw' in several of our modern senses; here it is linking two metaphors, being, one may suppose, suggested by the first, and suggesting the second. *Green* is the normal word for an unhealed wound (l. 125), and is also applicable to an untrained horse.

II. iii. 30. *the queen's kindred haughty and proud*; so Q. F cures the metre in an obvious enough way, *the queen's sons and brothers haught and proud*. I suspect rather that a monosyllabic adjective has dropped out after *haughty*.

II. iii. 40–45. Another typical 'block' of alterations: for *souls, dread, almost reason, fear, times, Ensuing dangers,* F reads: *hearts, fear, reason almost, dread, days, Pursuing danger.*

II. iv. (S.D.); this looks as though Q were again trying to economise in actors, and have only one 'Cardinal' for both this and the next scene, *i.e.* Cardinal Bourchier, Archbishop of Canterbury. Historically, two ecclesiastics are wanted, one to give up the great seal, as in this scene, who was Rotherham, Archbishop of York, but not a cardinal, and the other to advise Elizabeth, as in III. i., to give up the Duke of York, who was Bourchier, Archbishop of Canterbury and a cardinal. More, followed by Holinshed (though not by Hall), added to the possibilities of confusion by making Elizabeth's adviser both Archbishop of York and a cardinal.

II. iv. 1–2. F transposes the proper names (rewriting the second line for metre), thereby securing a correspondence (more or less) with history at the cost of probability and dramatic consistency. It is true that Edward first went, unexpectedly, through Northampton to Stony Stratford, and then back to Northampton. But Rotherham was not supposed to know of this unusual manœuvre, and in any case it seems to me absurd to suppose that Shakespeare would have deliberately introduced this piece of puzzling correctness, which would distract the attention of an audience as much as, say, the statement, 'Yes, they were in Dover last night, they'll be in Calais to-night, and in town to-morrow.' This alteration bears all over it the mark of the pernickety editor.

II. iv. 25. F has the much improved metre *To touch his growth nearer than he did mine.*

II. iv. 37 (S.D.). *Enter Dorset*; so Q. F has *Enter a Messenger*. This squares with More, and the speeches seem more suitable to a messenger.

II. iv. 53. *lawless*; so Q. If right, it must mean 'that can no longer enforce law'; F reads *aweless*, perhaps rightly.

III. i. 82. *formal vice, Iniquity*; i.e. 'like the Vice (who might be called a specific vice, such as Covetousness, or Iniquity in general) in the old Moralities, produce a *double entendre.*'

III. ii. 72. *upon the bridge*; i.e. on London Bridge, where the heads of executed traitors were placed.

III. ii. 96 (S.D.). *Hastings*; the pursuivant's name is recorded as Hastings. F omits it, presumably to avoid confusion, and reads *How now, sirrah?* for *Well met, Hastings*, and *fellow* for *Hastings* in l. 108.

III. ii. 111. *Sir John*; a common generic appellation for a priest.

III. iii. 23. *Make haste . . .* ; F, having used up the Q reading in l. 8, has to contrive something equivalent here.

III. iv. 79. *Now, by Saint Paul . . .* ; F reads:

> *Now by Saint Paul I swear*
> *I will not dine until I see the same.*
> *Lovel and Ratcliff, see that it be done.*

Q saves two actors in this scene. Its opening stage-direction is simply *Enter the Lords to Council*; here Lovel and Ratcliff disappear, Catesby appears instead of them in the immediately following stage-direction and instead of F's Ratcliff in l. 96 speech-heading.

III. v. (S.D.); no one seems to think that the F stage-direction needs any explanation. But why should the two great dukes suddenly appear in rotten armour?

III. v. 23 (S.D.). Q in this passage gets into trouble through economising. Catesby cannot both be conducting the execution of Hastings and fetching the Mayor; so ll. 12 and 13 disappear, and so does he from the Mayor's entry. However, he takes the place of Ratcliff and Lovel in l. 23 and the following stage-direction. All which would be well enough if it were not that in l. 19 he is told to o'erlook the walls!

III. v. 53–4. *I never . . . Shore*; F gives these two lines and the whole speech of Richard's which follows, to *Buck*.

III. v. 59. *hear*; Q and F both read *heard*, but this is probably an *e:d* error for *heare*.

III. vii. 131. *Your gracious self* . . . ; so Q, an obviously hyper-metric line; F no doubt cures the metre but at the cost of re-dundance, since *thereof* is just what is wanted after *This noble isle* 6 lines above, whereas F expands to:

> *Your gracious self to take on you the charge*
> *And kingly government of this your land*

One suspects that the right reading made

> *To take on you the sovereignty thereof*

one line, and that the preceding line ended in some such fashion as *we here solicit you*, or *we beg your gracious self*, which by some misunderstanding of corrections appeared as in Q.

III. vii. 186. *lustful eye*; F appears to object to *lustful*, since in III. v. 86 it emends to *raging*, and here to *wanton*; though to adjust the balance it alters *listed* in III. v. 87 to *lusted*.

III. vii. 219. F is obliged to omit this characteristic line, since it cannot allow Buckingham to swear in the preceding line, and reads *we will* for *'zounds! I'll*.

IV. i. (S.D.). *leading* . . . *daughter*; the brackets enclosing this portion of the stage-direction are not strictly accurate, since the words occur in neither F nor Q, but they, or something like them, seem to be demanded by the second line of the scene, which is only in F, and modern editors have followed Theobald in insert-ing them. Though why F should introduce an entirely silent and unnecessary child no one has explained.

IV. i. 29–30. *I do* . . . *do it*; so Q. F, more regularly but less vigorously:

> *No, madam, no; I may not leave it so:*
> *I am bound by oath, and therefore pardon me.*

IV. i. 53. *To meet* . . . *you*; F alters to produce a most un-necessary couplet:

> *In your behalf to meet you on the way.*

IV. ii. 8–9. *O Buckingham* . . . *indeed*; these two lines probably aside.

IV. ii. 46–9. *How now! . . . abides*; here the usual divergence is reversed and F has a version which is not only less complete, but hopelessly unmetrical (though a different line division, at *Lord* and *fled*, would make the latter part of it metrical):

> *How now, Lord Stanley, what's the news?*
> *Know, my loving lord, the Marquess Dorset,*
> *As I hear, is fled to Richmond*
> *In the parts where he abides.*

This passage could, no doubt, be used as an argument to support the view that F was printed from a corrected copy of a Quarto, the correction being cramped in the margin and the lines consequently misdivided.

IV. iii. 30. *But how . . . know.* F's reading is an excellent example of the kind of error that may arise from slovenly memory:

> *But where (to say the truth) I do not know.*

IV. iv. 4. *adversaries*; a comparison of this line with III. ii. 52 is a good illustration of the apparent causelessness of many of the differences between Q and F. F here reads *enemies*, but in the earlier line reads *adversaries* for Q's *enemies*.

IV. iv. 115. *neck*; F reads *head*, but in V. i. 25 reads *neck* for Q's *head*.

IV. iv. 138. *I hear his drum*; so Q. F reads *The trumpet sounds.* In the following stage-direction Q provides both instruments, F neither.

IV. iv. 178. *Humphrey Hour*; a mysterious phrase of which no really satisfactory explanation has been suggested. It is natural to suppose that it is some kind of pun on the phrase 'to dine with Duke Humphrey,' *i.e.* to spend a dinnerless dinner hour loitering in the nave of St. Paul's where there was a chapel to Humphrey, Duke of Gloucester. But it may be merely the name of a servant, or a topical allusion to which we have lost the clue.

IV. iv. 241. *So thrive I . . . arms*; so Q, a duplicate of ll. 404–5, where it fits the metre. F reads:

> *Madam, so thrive I in my enterprise,*
> *And dangerous success of bloody wars.*

IV. iv. 264. *from thy soul*; the Queen is playing on the two meanings, 'from the depth of thy soul' and 'away from,' *i.e.* with no love at all.

IV. iv. 365. *in plain terms tell her*; so Q. F has the weak alternative *plainly to her tell*.

IV. iv. 396. *for time past wrong'd by thee*; so F, accepted with some hesitation for Q's *for time, by the past wrong'd*.

IV. iv. 402. *Misus'd ere us'd . . .* ; so Q. F reads *by times ill-us'd repast*, which seems to be an attempt at emending. I think that the true reading is probably lost, since *misus'd o'erpast* looks like a misprint for *misus'd ere past*, i.e. variant on *Misus'd ere us'd*.

IV. iv. 429. *I buried*; so Q 1. This reading has been much too readily rejected for F's *I bury* or the later Qq *I'll bury*. To bury them *now* is just what he is not going to do: on the contrary, he is going to resurrect them (or others like them) from her daughter's womb in which he says he then buried them.

V. iii. (S.D.). Q dispenses with Surrey, makes Rutland address Catesby in l. 2 (where F reads: *My lord of Surrey, why look you so sad?*), and gives l. 3 to Catesby instead of Surrey.

V. iii. 241. HIS ORATION . . . ; this mysterious headline, like the similar one for Richard later, seems to imply that he either has said, or is supposed to have said, more than is printed, and the words which follow (as again with Richard) read not as the whole oration but as the peroration.

V. iv. (S.D.). Neither Q nor F gives any entry for Norfolk. The editors not unnaturally introduce him to be talked at. But it is at least possible for Catesby to be shouting at a Norfolk 'off,' and it is worth noticing that in 2 *Henry IV*, III. i. both Q and F, so far from introducing the Page who is addressed in the first three lines, emphasise his absence by giving *Enter King Henry solus*, as though he gave the order as he entered to a Page standing 'off.'

Glossary

MANY words and phrases in Shakespeare require glossing, not because they are in themselves unfamiliar, but for the opposite reason, that Shakespeare uses in their Elizabethan and unfamiliar sense a large number of words which seem so familiar that there is no incentive to look for them in the glossary. It is hoped that a glossary arranged as below will make it easy to see at a glance what words and phrases in any particular scene require elucidation. A number of phrases are glossed by what seems to be, in their context, the modern equivalent rather than by lexicographical glosses on the words which compose them.

Act First

SCENE I

line

6 MONUMENTS, memorials
9 FRONT, forehead
10 BARBED, armed
19 FEATURE, figure
   DISSEMBLING, cheating, *or perhaps*, mis-assembling
24 PIPING, *i.e.* when the pastoral pipe is heard
32 INDUCTIONS, (?) preparations
38 MEW'D, caged
44 TENDERING, in care for

line

55 CROSS-ROW, alphabet (*from having a cross prefixed in primers*)
60 TOYS, trifles
61 COMMIT, *sc.* to prison
66 OF WORSHIP, worshipful
83 GOSSIPS, 'familiars'
85 STRAITLY, strictly
106 ABJECTS, humble servants
110 ENFRANCHISE, free
115 LIE, *pun on* (*a*) lie in prison, (*b*) tell lies

SCENE II

3 OBSEQUIOUSLY, as a mourner
5 KEY-COLD, as cold as a key, *i.e.* very cold (*a phrase of the time, where we should say* clay-cold)

22 PRODIGIOUS, monstrous
49 CURST, shrewish
58 EXHALES, draws out
78 DEFUS'D, (?) shapeless (diffused)

123

Act I Sc. ii—*continued*

line		line	
94	FALCHION, curved sword	235	BARS, impediments
117	TIMELESS, untimely	250	MOIETY, half
120	EFFECT, executor	252	DENIER, coin of small value
151	BASILISK, serpent reputed to turn men to stone	261	IN, into
211	DESIGNS, preoccupations	264	SHADOW, image

SCENE III

line		line	
36	ATONEMENT, reconciliation	164	WHAT MAK'ST THOU, what are you doing
48	COG, cheat		
53	JACKS, knaves	177	CLOUT, napkin
61	LEWD, ignorant	206	STALL'D, installed
82	NOBLE, gold coin	241	FLOURISH, decoration
83	CAREFUL, full of cares		MY FORTUNE, fortune which by right is mine
89	DRAW ME IN SUSPECTS, include me in suspicions	255	MALAPERT, impertinent
102	I WIS, truly	264	AERY, brood (of bird of prey)
108	WITH THIS CONDITION, on these terms	314	FRANK'D UP TO FATTING, fattened in a 'frank,' *i.e.* sty (*cf. 'stalled ox'*)
139	MEED, reward		
	MEW'D, caged	317	SCATHE, harm
144	CACODEMON, evil spirit	328	BEWEEP, mourn for
159	PILL'D, pillaged		GULLS, fools

SCENE IV

line		line	
13	CITED UP, recalled	199	UNRIP'DST, tore open
45	GRIM FERRYMAN, *i.e.* Charon	202	DEAR, drastic
75	BREAKS, confounds	214	GALLANT-SPRINGING, in the May of youth
145	TALL FELLOW, 'stout fellow'	215	NOVICE, youth
146	GEAR, business	221	MEED, reward
147	COSTARD, head	240	LABOUR, labour for
148	CHOP, shove	258	FLATTERER, deceiver
175	EVIDENCE, witnesses		
176	QUEST, jury		

Act Second

SCENE I

line		line	
44	TO MAKE THE PERFECT PERIOD, to round off (to put the full stop to)	57	HARDLY BORNE, resented
		91	LAG, tardily
		95	CURRENT, *met. from coins*

SCENE II

line	*line*
18 INCAPABLE, unreasoning	120 TRAIN, *sc.* of attendants
22 IMPEACHMENTS, charges	127 ESTATE, state
28 VIZARD, mask	142 POST, haste
47 INTEREST, share	144 CENSURES, judgments
60 MOIETY, fraction	148 SORT OCCASION, fix a suitable
81 PARCELL'D, particular	opportunity
95 REQUIRES, asks payment of	149 INDEX, first step in
110 BUTT-END, 'tag-end'	151 CONSISTORY, council-chamber
112 CLOUDY, mournful	

SCENE III

15 NONAGE, minority	41 CANNOT ALMOST, can
27 EMULATION, rivalry	scarcely
29 DANGER, power to harm	

SCENE IV

20 GRACIOUS, full of grace	35 SHREWD, smart
24 MY UNCLE'S GRACE, my un-	52 JET, encroach upon
cle, his Grace	55 MAP, panorama
35 PARLOUS, *contr. of* perilous,	
i.e. precocious (*'l'enfant*	
terrible')	

Act Third

SCENE I

4 CROSSES, hitches	118 LIGHT, trifling
11 JUMPETH, corresponds	126 CROSS, perverse
22 SLUG, sluggard	132 PROVIDED, ready
31 INDIRECT, contrary	152 INCENSED, incited
34 PRESENTLY, immediately	154 PERILOUS, *see gloss on* II. iv.
71 RE-EDIFIED, built on to	35
94 LIGHTLY, usually	155 CAPABLE, receptive
103 IDLE, worthless	180 DIVIDED, separate
114 TOY, trifle	201 DIGEST, work out

SCENE II

11 RAZ'D, torn off	46–47 FORWARD UPON HIS PARTY,
25 INSTANCE, evidence	active on his side
26 FOND, foolish	55 TO THE DEATH, even if I die
29 INCENSE, incite	for it
44 FOUL, *adv.*	

Act III   Sc. ii—*continued*

line

63 PACKING, about their business

97 PRESENTLY, immediately

line

103 SUGGESTION, instigation

116 SHRIVING WORK, absolution

SCENE III

11 CLOSURE, enclosure

23 EXPIATE, run out

SCENE IV

8 INWARD WITH, in the counsels of

14 NEAR IN LOVE, in close confidence

25 NEGLECT, cause neglect of

28 PRONOUNC'D YOUR PART, acted as your understudy

41 AS, that

42 WORSHIPFUL, with feelings of respect

48 PROLONG'D, postponed

84 FOND, foolish

87 FOOT-CLOTH, caparisoned

91 PURSUIVANT, herald

SCENE V

9 INTENDING, pretending

35 CONVERSATION, dealings with

36 LAID FROM, was free from
SUSPECT, suspicion

58 PREVENTED, anticipated

64 MISCONSTER, misinterpret
IN, in the case of

72 OF OUR INTENTS, for our intentions

76 IN ALL POST, in all haste

77 MEET'ST ADVANTAGE OF THE TIME, when opportunity best serves

78 INFER, bring in the point of

83 LUXURY, lasciviousness

87 LISTED, wished

88 FOR A NEED, if need arises

111 TAKE SOME PRIVY ORDER, arrange secretly

SCENE VI

2 ENGROSS'D, written out

7 PRECEDENT, rough-copy

SCENE VII

8 ENFORCEMENT, violation

9 TYRANNY FOR, (?) tyrannical temper in

13 IDEA, copy

15 LAID OPEN, discoursed on

45 INTEND, pretend

46 BUT WITH, except after

49 GROUND . . . DESCANT, theme and variations on it

55 LEADS, roof

76 ENGROSS, fatten

112 DISGRACIOUS, unpleasing

127 GRAFT, grafted

128 SHOULDER'D IN, thrust into

134 SUCCESSIVELY, in succession

174 RESPECTS, grounds
NICE, over-scrupulous

210 EFFEMINATE, womanly
REMORSE, pity

224 ENTREATS, entreaties

232 MERE ENFORCEMENT, downright compulsion
ACQUITTANCE, acquit

Act Fourth

SCENE I

line	*line*
11 GRATULATE, greet	61 VERGE, circlet
19 STRAITLY, strictly	67 HUMOUR, mood
33 LOOKER ON, spectator (*i.e.* of their 'queenship')	99 TEEN, sorrow

SCENE II

8 PLAY THE TOUCH, apply the touchstone	75 DISTURBS, disturbers
29 UNRESPECTIVE, thoughtless	94 MOVEABLES, possessions
41 PRESENTLY, immediately	118 JACK, figure on a clock which strikes the bell
42 WITTY, quick-witted	128 FEARFUL, apprehensive

SCENE III

6 FLESH'D, having tasted blood	31 AFTER SUPPER, dessert (*cf. 'afternoon'*)
18 REPLENISHED, completely finished	54 EXPEDITION, speed
19 PRIME CREATION, first day of creation	

SCENE IV

5 INDUCTION, introduction	176 COMFORTABLE, bringing comfort
39 SIGNORY, seniority	180 DISGRACIOUS, displeasing
56 EXCELLENT, outstanding	204 MOE, more (*Eliz. plural*)
68 BOOT, make-weight	220 OPPOSITE, contrary
72 ADULTERATE, debased	222 UNAVOIDED, unavoidable
74 INTELLIGENCER, go-between	227 COZEN'D, cheated
75 FACTOR, agent	256 so, provided that
84 BOTTLED, bloated	LETHE, river of oblivion
87 PRESENTATION, *i.e. on the stage*	259 PROCESS, setting forth
88 INDEX, prologue	275 HUMOUR, temper
92 SIGN, emblem	349 INFER, make a point of
130 WINDY, garrulous	367 QUICK, 'smart' (*Q.E. puns in next line on meaning 'alive'*)
131 SUCCEEDERS, heirs	
138 EXCLAIMS, exclamations	
139 EXPEDITION, hasty progress	372 GEORGE, the figure which is the pendant of the Collar of the Garter
160 CONDITION, character	
171 TETCHY, fractious	
173 PRIME OF, early	GARTER, Order of Garter
174 AGE CONFIRM'D, full manhood	408 OPPOSITE, contrary

Act IV   Sc. iv—*continued*

line		line	
411	TENDER, be tender of	456	PRESENTLY, quickly
419	ATTORNEY, go-between	504	ASSURANCE, security
444	HULL, drift	510	MOE, more

SCENE V

3	FRANK'D, in a sty	16	MOE, more

Act Fifth

SCENE III

line		line	
11	BATTALION, army	242	THE LEISURE AND ENFORCE-MENT, the compulsion of the lack of leisure
24	MODEL, scheme		
54	BEAVER, helmet		
69	STAVES, shafts of lances	254	STONE, (imitation) jewel
74	COCK-SHUT TIME, twilight (*deriv. uncertain*)	262	FAT, wealth
		269	RANSOM, forfeit
109	PEISE, weigh	283	BRAV'D, dared (*i.e.* risen in)
139	FALL, let fall	304	WINGED, flanked
	EDGELESS, blunted	318	INFERR'D, set out
150	COUSINS, *general word of 'kinship,' here* nephews	334	FOND, foolish
		338	BOBB'D, struck
		345	WELKIN, sky

SCENE V

36	REDUCE, bring back